'BIG RANCH' COWBOY

Other Work by Red Cloud Wolverton

'Stagecoach 76'
'To The Far Corners'
'Cowboy Coogan'
'The Devil's Garden' – (short story published in 'Tales From Cowboy Country' compilation)
'JimmyKane' (short story published in 'Good Medicine' compilation)
'A Cowboy's Ranch' and **'Hopi'** published in 'Tales From Out There' – Range Magazine publication

'BIG RANCH' COWBOY

By
'Red Cloud' Wolverton

Illustrated by Margery Wolverton

Edited by Wendy Wolverton

© 2022 Wendy Wolverton all rights reserved

No portion of this book may be copied or duplicated without author's permission.

Book format & layout: Wendy Wolverton

ISBN 978-1-7378192-2-6 (printed)
ISBN 978-1-7378192-3-3 (Ebook)

Copyright Library of Congress 2022
Published and printed in the United States of America

Preface

75 Years, a Cowboy!

For years, I would think about something I'd been involved in, and how I reacted to it. I'd think about how I might have done it different.

I started telling friends about my escapades, until I was asked several times why I didn't write about them; so at night, after we were through with the day's work; if I wasn't too tired, I'd sit down and write what we had done that day.

I wrote about many events, but never showed then to anyone.

One day, my wife asked me why I didn't write about them.

"I did! There's an old red suitcase full of them, that I have written through the years!" She wanted to see them and became very interested.

She had an old typewriter, and started typing them out for me. It took her most of a year to get them all printed out. That was many years ago.

Finally, this last January, she got them out, and started putting them in book form; so we could get them published.

So, here are the yarns. Hope you enjoy them!
R.C.

Dedication

    Most of my dedications go to some old time cowboys talking in a restaurant one night, about the big chuckwagon ranches still running in the Far West.

    And to my oldest sister that insisted I should go to college, with only two years of high school behind me. I did, and got a two year diploma, an Associate Degree in Science.

    But most of all, to my wife, that struggled through pages of faded out hand written yarns about my past escapades.

    There is very little poetic license in these yarns. Most of it is close to how it all took place.

Red Cloud

8

Table of Contents

Preface   5
Dedication   7
Cowboy Lingo   12

SECTION I   13

(Early Years 1929-1950's - The Northwest, Drifting Cowboy, The Big Ranches)

Photos - Family he grew up in	14
All I Ever Wanted	17
My Early Years	21
Arkansas River Canyon	29
A Drifting Cowboy	31
Santa Rosa	35
Santa Rosa Parade	37
ZX Ranch	39
New Handle	47
A Cowboy's Outfit	49
Horseshoeing	52
The Smile of Fortune	55
Elko Nevada	57
Vermejo Park	59
Mules At Vermejo, New Mexico Gentrys	
Happy Hobo	65
The Devil's Garden	67
Laughing Cowboys	87
A Tough Break	89
A Strong Corral	95
Wrap and Tangle	97
Jack and Casper	99
Lonesome Cowboy	105
Slinghead Brown	107
Cowboys and Buckaroos	111
A Gallopin' Goose	116
A Good Cook and a Mule Skinner	117
Chuckwagon Cook	119
Ranch Cookin'	121
Wagon Cook	123
El Bingo, The Wagon Jingler	127

Where A Cowboy Spends His Pastime	129
The Last Lynching	131
Spanish Omelet	133
Goodby	135

SECTION II — 137

(Middle Years 1950's -1970's, Montana and Colorado, Education, Marriage, Family)

A Hot Spot On A Cold Night	139
Hopi	141
Bronc Riding	147
Monotonous	149
Letter to Jarretts	151
A Cowboy's Education	153
To Mrs. Stinson	154
Summertime Romance	157
My Heart	161
Just Riding Along	162
A Cowboy's Ranch	165
East Or West?	176
Marge in Montana	179
The Colorado Rockies	182
Time to Move	183
A Whale of an Adjustment	187
Var La Baine (Forever)	191
Bedroll Cowboy	193
A Cowboy's Romance	197
My Darling	199
At The Local Waterhole	203
The Privy	210
Not Quite Broke	211
Red's Log 1957	213
And the Wind Blew	229
I Did It Once; So Now I have To Do It Again	231
Red Roses	241
Letter To Margie	242
The Shining Star	244
What Goes Around, Comes Around	248
Mountain Meadow	253
All In A Day's Work	259

SECTION III 265

(The Later Years -1970's-2000'S, The Southwest, Horses, Stagecoaches, Movies)

Application For A Job	267
The Inaugural Parade	273
Apacheland	287
Horse Whispering	293
Introduction To Old Tucson	295
Morgans In the Movies	297
Destry, A Good Horse	301
Smart Horse -Suntan	309
'Stagecoach Movie'	311
Our Stagecoach Harness	315
Hatch, New Mexico	319
Outstanding Events In My Life	321
The Distance Between	327
Adios	328
About the Author and Illustrator	335

Cowboy Lingo

CANDY WAGON – vehicle that hauled food and supplies to the line camps

CAVVY – horse herd

DALLIES – takes turns around the horn with a lass rope

DOUGH GODS – doughy biscuits cooked in grease

GREENBROKE – (horse) – half trained, or just started

GUNSEL – tenderfoot or novice

HOULIHAN – var. hoolihan – a special type of backhand throw which cowboys use, especially for catching horses, with a small loop

JIGGER BOSS – second in command under the wagon boss if there is one, or if not, then under the cow boss

JINGLER - wagon wrangler or horse wrangler

LATIGO – leather strap that holds the cinch to the saddle

LEPPY CALF – orphan calf

REMUDA – herd of horses held in a corral, usually a rope corral

RIATA – leather lass rope, as from the Vaqueros

RIGGIN' – saddle, in rodeo terms, the bronc saddle or bareback leather straps that the rider hangs on to

ROSINJAW - all ranch hands, other than the cowboys or buckaroos

SECTION – (of land = 640 acres)

SHANK'S PONY – on foot

SOOGANS – bed rolls

SURPOGULATED – thought, contemplated

TRACKIN' – moving a horse one or two steps out of the tracks where he stood while being saddled

WADDY - cowboy

SECTION I

- Early Years 1929-1950's
- The Northwest
- The 'Big Ranches'

RED CLOUD
The family he grew up in

Red and Ernie

Edwin Pueblo at about 1944

RED CLOUD

All I Ever Wanted

All I ever wanted was to be a cowboy.

I was born in 1929, in Kansas City, Kansas. I growed up for a while in a little community where the merchants got together in the summer time, and would put on a free outdoor movie; sort of like the modern drive ins, except everybody sat on chairs or laid on the grass, and watched that movie on a canvas screen.

The westerns were what took my eye. If I go back a little further, I can tell about the first movie I ever saw. The cowboy hero of that movie was the first hero I ever had. That was Buck Jones in "Red River Valley."

I've pulled many a sweaty saddle blanket off my horse since then. I don't think I ever spent a full day ahorseback, that something exciting, funny, or unusual didn't happen. Before the full day ended, some happenings were downright hilarious, and some were pretty western. All the "western" incidents with horses, weren't with saddle horses. Some were with harness horses on farm machinery and wagons. Some with stagecoaches.

I think I was eight years old, the first summer I took a team to the field. Of course, I was a lot older than that; being pretty near nine, as my birthday is in September!

I'm not saying I was handling snorty horses then, but what I'm trying to get across is that I did have a lot of horse driving experience by the time I had my first real, for sure, goodness, wild run away at the mature age of 12 years!

Two years to an older man, when you're looking back, don't seem to have been a very long time; but two years from, say 12 to 14, is an eternity at that age. What I'm trying to say, is by the time I was 14, I'd had a lot of experience. Several runaways, and a few bucking horse rides. Enough so that I developed from an ordinary "punkin' rollin'" kid, to quite a bronc stomping cowboy.

I'd had my "Tony" horse, and had gotten him going pretty good. It was time to progress from Tom Mix to Will James. Incidentally, for those of you that don't understand what I've said, "Tony" was the name of the beautiful black horse that Tom Mix rode for so many years through the Silver Screen escapades.

There was another "Tony" horse in my life, but my first one, was my first love. He was a beautiful, shiny, coal black, part Morgan, with long flowing mane and tail. He had a magnificent white stripe on his face and three white stockings. To a 12 year old cowboy, he was everything in the world.

Then along came "Smoky,"

My first "Tony" was the "Black Beauty" of my life; but Smoky was the first real challenge to my cowboy life.

The first time I saw him at a horse sale, I fell in love. It was a cold March day, but we were there early. My dad and I needed plenty of time to look over the young horses. I'd had to sell Tony the previous fall, but now we could afford another horse, if we could find one reasonably priced. Thatchers, a neighbor, were having a horse dispersal sale. They had a lot of horses there, that day; several hundred head. There were mares, colts, broncos, and green broke horses, as well as finished cowhorses.

We'd looked over several corrals full, when we found the horse for me. I don't know who saw him first, but we both, my dad and I, were satisfied we'd found the right horse when we saw him.

He had conformation, size, a good eye, good sound legs and feet, big enough to pack him, but sure not a "puddin' foot."

And color! Well, he had it. The color that gave him his name, before we even got a chance to bid on him. Old "Smoky."

He was a beautiful smoky blue-gray, with dappled tones; and what really set him off was the two white spots on his neck on the near side, and the one spot on his near ribs. All the spots were sort of jagged and irregular shaped, but something like four or five inches up and down, and eight or ten inches long. He had the hint of a little white on his forehead, and one white foot, but the rest of him was a steel blue roan, and hard as iron.

He was unmarked, unbroken, and a three year old. He sure had class, and a sense of independence. He wasn't about to let no human get any closer to him, than what the stout railroad tie corrals forced him to.

I spent most of the morning down by the corral, planning his breaking. I could just see me galloping across the plains on his sleek back.

Life doesn't always go as we plan it, especially back in the days when you could buy a whale of a good finished saddle horse for $125.00 to $150.00. It took quite a good bronco to bring $50.00. We had about $75.00 we could spend on a horse for me.

Several head sold before "Smoky" came in. They had sold at a good price, but well within the limit we could afford. I knew for sure we'd be hauling "Smoky" home in our old truck that afternoon.

There must have been several people there that day that liked my horse. I was about knocked flat. The bidding started on him about where it quit on the best of the previous ones. "Smoky" sold for $125.00.

My dad had to quit bidding on him, long before that. When the auctioneer hollered "Sold!" My dad turned to me with a very beaten look and said, maybe we can get another one, but I think he felt the same as I did that day. There just wasn't another horse there we really wanted. At least I don't recall him bidding on any of the others.

My Early Years

Most of my life I've worked with horses of one kind or another. I think it was the summer I was seven, my dad said I'd laid around long enough; it was time I learned to work. He put me on a dump rake behind a team. We did all our ranching and farming with horses back in those days. Seems as though my dad was always buying or trading, or taking horses to break for their use.

Somewhere around 1932, we moved from a ranch near Center, Colorado to wind up in Kansas City, Kansas. Things were tough, but my dad had worked in the Kansas City stockyards in the past. He knew who to get ahold of to go to work there.

Somehow before 1936, some land investors talked my dad in taking over a stock farm near Oak Grove, Missouri, to get it in shape so they could sell it. The place covered over a section of country; a large stock farm for Missouri. By sometime in 1939, the investors figured how to move it at a profit. Pop started looking for a better stock farm to take over. About 30 miles away, he located a real good place of about one-half a section to take over.

As soon as the summer crops were taken care of, we started moving. Along in October, Pop decided my uncle (young, but older than me) and I could drive two teams and two wagons, to the new place. We'd both been over the route two or three times, moving stuff with Pop in his old 1935 Ford truck; so we knew the route.

It was cold in the early morning when we got hooked up and started out. Ed, my uncle, took the lead with a team of big, ambitious, stout, young horses that Pop had started that year. My team was about 13 or 1400 pound mares that Pop had started to break after we first moved to the farm. We were about half way and getting colder steadily.

We were driving in a jog or slow trot. Ed was about to freeze; so he decided he could get out of his wagon, with his lines in hand, and run along beside to get warm. We'd gone quite a ways that way, when I don't know what happened, but instantly, Ed's team was in a dead run, and the lines were jerked out of Ed's hands!

My team sold out right behind his! Two teams and wagons running at a good pace without a driver on the lead wagon! We were coming up onto a sort of flat hill. Having been over the route before, I remembered thinking the road curved over the rise, down the hill, and made a sharp turn at the bottom across a bridge.

Something had to be done.

Ed's big horses were getting a little tired or winded. There was a good wide grassy bar pit about 30 feet or wider between the road and a fence. My team was really enjoying their run. I decided I could swing to the left of Ed's team and get ahead of them enough to cause them to pull into the bar pit area. Maybe it'd be soft enough to stop or slow the team down, to where I might crowd them over to the fence where they might stop.

I got ahead of his team and had them crowded into the middle of the bar pit. One of Ed's team stumbled and was falling as I heard a noise behind me. There was Ed hanging on the right running board of a Model A Ford. Ed bailed off that outfit at a dead run and got to his team while they were fighting the world to get going again.

He got them under control and settled down. I ran my team on into the bar pit toward the fence. Before we hit, I got them stopped. We got all lined up again, with Ed in the lead. For some reason, with me in behind Ed's wagon, my team would snort and try to run past Ed. I couldn't stop them, but I could still guide them. I'd just cram them into the back of Ed's wagon. My neck yoke was hitting the tail gate in the back of Ed's wagon.

We made it on to the next farm without any more serious trouble, but the rear of Ed's wagon needed lots of repair after me following plowing into it several times.

A thrilling run for a 10 year old boy!

In February of 1943, my dad moved our family from the Missouri farm, to a small ranch west of Pueblo, Colorado, along the Arkansas River. He had worked for a horse trader for several years before World War I, and he started the same business in Pueblo; only doing it himself instead of working for someone else.

From the time I was young, my dad was a horse trader. Every week he'd go to the big horse sales and bring home 2 or 3 or more, old broke horses. There were many ranches at that time that were going through a change. There weren't enough younger men that could handle those old cranky rough string horses any more. They were all in the military service. My older brother had joined up when he was 17, right after graduating from high school.

I turned 13 in the fall of that year. He immediately started me on those snorty horses to get them gentle for a riding stable string which he started. There were a number of those old "gentle cowhorses," we'd have to tie up a foot; and some we had to throw and tie their feet together, to get them saddled. More than a few, we tied down and saddled, my paw would tell me, "Get ready, a-straddle of him, and come up with him, when I take the foot ropes off!"

Some didn't come up gentle! One fired me away so high, my dad said, "If I'd known you were going so high, I'd have jacked up the barn and moved it over, so you wouldn't have so far to fall!"

One, a blue roan, bucked me across its neck, ahead of my saddle, before it threw me skyward. After some fighting and jousling, I was finally able to get back on without getting pawed or kicked. I hooked a spur in a blood vein behind its ear, when I was heading upward. The blood was spurting out so bad, we had to fore-foot him and lay him down to get it stopped. When we finally got it stopped, Paw looked at me and says, "What now?"

"Let it up. I'm ready. Open the Gate!"
Away across the prairie we went about ten miles or more. Suddenly I had to "go" or wet my pants. I got my horse's head doubled up, and stepped off him. I was able to hang on to my caballo. To get back on became a problem, with him pawing and kicking at me.

I'd pulled my right rein across the saddle in getting off. Luckily I had long split reins and was finally able to get his mouth pulled up, and get a wrap around the horn with one rein. With his head pulled around like that, he wasn't able to see me with his kicking and his striking.

I was able to get a good grip of the horn with my right hand, and in between him striking at me with his front feet, and kicking jumps from behind, I was able to vault back in the saddle. I was younger and more agile then. With his scotched nose almost in my lap, I was able to get square back in place to have a good show at him when I turned his head loose. After a couple jumps skyward, I got him back in a lope and made it back to camp, with a half broke horse!

By the time I was 15, I could ride a pretty salty pony. Pop thought the proper way to start an unbroken horse was to forefoot him, jerk him down, tie their feet together, roll them in a saddle; then get me in the middle of them, jerk the ropes free, and I'd come up with them. A half day later, I had a pretty well-started horse, even if he wasn't broke to get on or off of.

My dad had 40 or 50 or more horses all the time. One of them was a big smooth-mouthed bay, about 1,200 pounds and close to 16 hands tall. We had a bucking chute in the side of our big round corral. A lot of the horses that we were sure were cranky, we'd lay them down, saddle them, and I'd come up with them. When I came out on this bay, my neighbor, more than a quarter mile away, told me he'd heard the worst awful bawling and ground battering he'd ever heard for a long time; before I rode it to a standstill.

If I could ride that way, why didn't I go into the Saddlebronc riding circuit? I might ride, but I couldn't show a'tall. If I could have learned how to ride and show a bucking horse, I'd have headed for the arena circuit. I've punched cows on horses that Saddlebronc riders would have been hard put to fit a ride on them. I could ride some of them out in the open, but I never learned to show a bucking horse in an arena.

One morning after I left for school, someone stopped by and told Dad they'd seen a bunch of our horses several miles up the river, in someone else's place. The only horse in the corral was this bay. I had put several rides on him, and had it where you could handle it some. Pop saddled him, and after a battle, took out after the strays. It was in the late winter. Chunks of ice were floating down the river. The horses were across on the other side.

Every time he got old Bay into the water up to the shoulders, with the ice floating down, old Bay would whirl and buck back to solid ground. The third time on solid ground, Pop spotted a water-logged limb about the size of a ball bat. That time when old Bay balked and tried to turn, Pop whacked it down across the top of his head, and cold-cocked old Bay.

Its nose and head was under the surface. Pop had to step off into that cold icy water and get its head and nose up to keep him from drowning. When Pop stood up, the water was over his belt. When he got back on old Bay, wet and soggy, the old cayuse baled right out into the icy drifting water to cross the river and get around the strays. All Pop said to me that night was, "Why didn't you keep a better broke horse up to wrangle on?"

"That's one way to get them broke gentle!" was my reply.

28

Draw N. of River Arkansas - now under water

1945

Arkansas River Canyon

This morning out in the canyon,
In the light of the flickering false dawn;
My soul was fully contented,
And my desire for leaving was gone.

The snowy white clouds hurry to the mountains,
And the winds whispered to the swaying pine trees.
A coyote called to his lonesome companion,
And an eagle sailed into the breeze.

I listened to the murmur of the river,
As the boulders held it up in its flight.
I know I shall always be happy,
When I dream of the Arkansas River,
In a Colorado Canyon at night.

I dreamed that dream as years went by;
My nights in Colorado in the mountains high.
You've gone away like the stars in the sky.
My life's in the West; so I'll bid you goodbye.

30

A Drifting Cowboy

I started my drifting along toward the end of World War II. I must have been about 15 years old. I'd stopped to get a bite to eat in a restaurant in western looking ranch country. Down a ways at a table, sat several "old time" looking cowboys. Men! They interested me, so I got to listening to their talk.

One big-hatted fellow was telling these other fellows, "If you want to work on an old time chuckwagon outfit, you should drift out in the Nevada, eastern Oregon, and southern Idaho country. There's several outfits out there that keep their chuckwagon crew year around." My ears were tingling. So many of my acquaintances had gone to war that never made it back. My older brother, Ernie, was one of those. I didn't crave that kind of end. I wanted to spend some time on one of those big spreads.

At the age of 15, school became unbearable. World War II had already claimed many other young fellows I knew. I couldn't live with the thought of staying in school until I was old enough for the service, and missing the outdoor life I yearned for, so I drifted.

I'd found some literature on ranches. There were still some big old time ranches in northern Nevada and southeastern Oregon; so that is where I headed. Those big ranches still used mules on their chuckwagons in 1944. The wagon crews spent from early in the spring until late in the fall on the range, with the cattle and horse roundups.

My buddy and I quit high school. We were sophomores, and we headed out west. About all we had was a couple old worn out saddles and bridles, run over boots, and pretty well used hats. We put together a couple California hotrolls. I didn't know then, they were called that. We dumped our outfits in my old '29 Chevy coupe, in the middle of the night, and headed west.

We got a few "day" jobs along the way. We landed a job feeding cattle until we had enough money to move on west. It's unbelievable, but the population of the state of Nevada was under 60,000 at that time. We made it over the mountains, but the jingle in our pockets was about gone; so I sold my car for $25.00, so we could get something to eat.

We rode the bus some. But our thumb, more. We were picked up as vagrants in a little town on the west slope of the mountains. The cop that picked us up hauled us around for a while on his regular beat. He finally said he was going to hang on to us until morning, but if we'd join the navy, he wouldn't throw us in jail. We agreed we'd probably do it. About this time, he got an urgent call to respond to, an attempted burglary. He took his car keys, but left us sitting in it; telling us he'd be right back. As soon as he was out of sight, we grabbed "shank's pony" and headed out of 'Dodge' so to speak. We hoofed it half way across the hills of California before we came up on a construction job where they needed a couple hands to run "Mexican draglines." Did you ever shovel gravel all day on an empty stomach? Then one of you rents a small sleeping room, where the other fellow slips in; and you both spend the night on a narrow cot to keep warm, with only one blanket for cover. I'd hate to live over some of those younger days.

More of that thumb type of travel. We finally wound up in San Francisco in a bus depot.

Sometimes the trick worked that you'd study the chart and find a bus that left sometime in the morning; so if you were questioned, you planned on leaving on that bus when the time came. We got out early in the morning and strolled down to the bay where we could see the Golden Gate Bridge and Alcatraz. We decided to walk across the bridge. There was some kind of a squabble going on, down on the "Rock," and there were a number of police and gunboats there. It was quite interesting to a young fellow from the high rough country of the Colorado Mountains. There was no place to turn back to; so we just kept heading north. We finally got a ride in the back of a pickup all the way to Santa Rosa, California, broke and hungry.

34

Santa Rosa

Another short night in the "Trailways" motel, and we were back out on the street trying to figure a way to get some breakfast. I checked through my pockets again and found a dime. Then I looked up at a restaurant sign and read, 'Coffee 5 cents.' We entered and ordered our breakfast. "Two cups of coffee, please." I plopped my dime down on the counter. We added lots of cream and sugar for our 'breakfast'.

We were enjoying our meal when this older cowboy-looking fellow came in behind and between us, and touched me gently on the shoulder. I turned around. He grinned and says, "S'cuse me, but I'm wondering if you boys would like a job breaking horses?" One look at him, and we were off our stools, grinning. I never asked how much it paid. I just said, "When do we go to work?"

I cherished all my life, working for Corey Kole, that old Nevada outlaw; and his wife. Those horses we broke were mostly gathered up in northwestern Nevada in the dark of the moon; then peddled to locals when we got them broke gentle. I learned a lot from him besides how to move a few horses. Corey was quite a horseman; the best I ever knew. In the early thirties, he'd leave Twin Falls in the spring when school was out, with a saddle and pack horse and supplies. He'd come back in the fall with enough broke mustangs he'd caught through the summer to put himself through another year of school.

In 1932, he went to Fort Sill, Oklahoma and joined the Cavalry to break horses. His basic training consisted of training him how to ride and school a cavalry horse. Those horses have to know all the basic dressage cues for the riders to keep them in formation. Many a good bronc stomper doesn't know a right lead from a cross lead; and any horse that had a tendency to turn on his front feet got a severe schooling. Corey was that way before he joined up, and I was that way before I went to work for him. Corey taught me a horse just wasn't broke if he didn't know and respond to the basic dressage cues.

Outlaws come in all shapes and sizes. They aren't all cowboys and ex-cowboys. A race-horse man I got acquainted with asked if I'd ride his horse for a while. It was OK with Corey. I started riding and fell in love with my first thoroughbred: a big black, 16-1 or 2 hands. Powerhouse. He'd had a bad habit of shying sideways when he was running on the track. For no apparent reason, I've had him shy, and at a hard run, jump half way across the track. He was getting rid of his jockeys when he'd do that; but I rode long, straight-legged; and he never managed to get away from me. When I could, I was quirting his underneath part on the off side when he hit the ground. He finally quit shying with me. One day on the one mile track, the owner said that I should have him wide open when I passed the 3/4 marker, and come on past the one mile marker full bore. I had already galloped him several miles, but he made that last quarter in 22 seconds. I finally found out why he was run only in low profile races. There was a bad race horse stable fire that past winter, and the owner had collected several thousand dollars on his horses that burned up in the fire. That old thoroughbred was one of the ones that had insurance policy coverage.

Santa Rosa Parade

While I was there, Corey got me involved in something that changed my life. The local people were planning their July 4th celebration with lots of enthusiasm. This included a parade, with one of the entries being an authentic stagecoach with a six horse hitch, and Hollywood stuntman Richard Farnsworth as the driver.

Corey was one of the members of the committee planning the day's entertainment. Someone came up with the idea of holding up the stagecoach during the parade, which was immediately approved. The rancher, our boss, offered our services as the varmints to do the 'dirty work'"

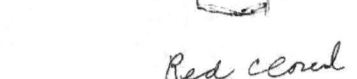
Red cloud

As the coach was traveling down the main street in front of all the crowd, the two of us came in ahorseback, with our faces masked with our wild rags, and a pistol (with blanks in it of course), in the other hand, making lots of noise, too. It was a very successful holdup. We got away with the 'gold.' However, there must have been a snitch somewhere. We weren't more than a block away along the parade route, when we were 'upheld' by the local sheriff and his posse!

There just happened to be a big log jail in a holding pen close by. Of course, there was a 'hanging judge' and cowboy jury already picked, waiting for us. We got tried and convicted in short order, and sentenced to be interned in the log cell.

Of course if someone could go our bail, we could get out, with the provision we had to ride around ahorseback and apprehend anyone that wasn't in western clothes; and that they looked like they might have enough dollars for their fine, (for not dressing properly) for the event. The money was to be donated to some local charity.

We finally persuaded some pretty girls we'd met, to go our bail. We had a lot of fun for the rest of the day, herding those dudes up before the 'Hanging Judge,' and adding their 'fines' to the local community.

After that episode, I've always been interested in stagecoach activities and showing them. That holdup was a great way to relive the old time stage coach days, and it left me with the idea that someday I would get one of my own; but that's another story.

After the parade, we got what colts Corey had broke to ride, and had a few dollars in our pockets. We decided to head north. Starting to drift.

Somewhere along the way, we'd heard about the ZX in Paisley, Oregon; so that's where we headed. When I was young, all I could dream of was that I wanted to be a 'big ranch cowboy'.

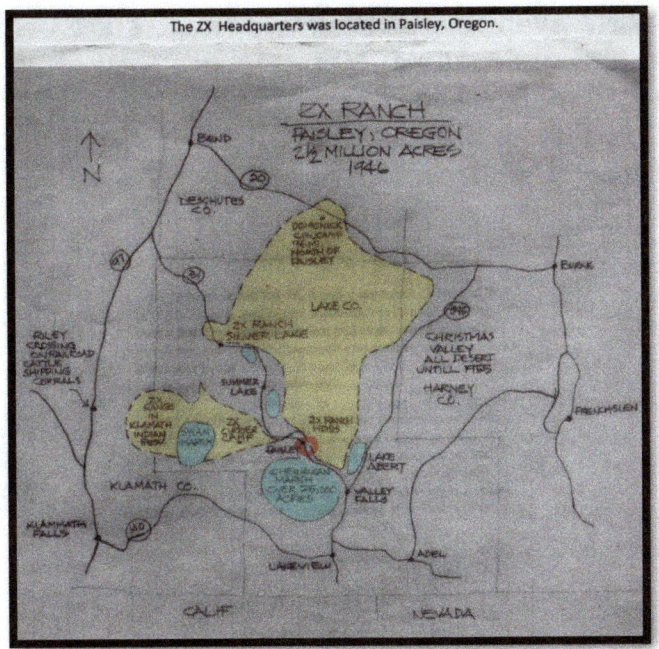

The ZX Headquarters was located in Paisley, Oregon.

ZX Ranch

When I found the ZX, it was a big ranch. It ranged in Lake, Deschutes, and Klamath counties in Oregon, grazing over 2.5 million acres of desert, mountain range, and winter meadows; and ran a chuckwagon and cowboy crew ahorseback year around. When I first worked there, the ZX ran about 20,000 productive mother cows.
I knew I'd found what I was wanting.

Six months, more or less of the year, the cowboys were busy trailing cattle from winter quarters to the desert. Then as summer approached, the cattle were trailed to the mountain range. Like in the earliest trail work, one herd after another was gathered and moved up to a hundred miles to the desert.

With several herds then, we would start gathering and trailing to the mountain range up to a hundred miles again, on most trails. Next, spend a couple months branding, sorting, and start shipping by railroad to market. Then trail what's left, the rest of the fall, to winter quarters, up to fifty or 75 miles away.

The six winter months, more or less, were spent sorting, moving, and shipping cattle until time to start shaping up the herds in late winter, to get ready to start the circle all over again.

Those six months of trailing cattle were shorter trails than the old time Texas drives, but ours added up as many miles as the Texas to Montana trails did in a season.

Towards the end of the war, the ranches were pretty shorthanded. The crews were made up mostly of the "pensioners," old, crippled, or stove up cowboys who had been put back to work, and the "buttons," pre-draft age!

The war had also created a horse problem. With most of the able bodied cowboys called away, there weren't many young horses "started," and many of the cranky ones weren't being used much. The gentle ponies were handed to the older fellows, and that was no more than right. The most of these older fellows had had their share of the falls and spills, and couldn't deliberately court any more.

Buster Vaughn was the super, and Hank McDaniels was the wagon boss. Most of the cattle were wintered on the Chewaucan Marsh at Paisley. The valley was about six or eight miles wide and 15 to 20 miles long. It wasn't all meadow. It lay in two sections; the Chewaucan and The Lower Marsh. Several other ranches had chunks of the country along the west side, and in the Lower Marsh.

The ZX hayed 30,000 acres, more or less, and this was the main winter quarters for most of the cattle.

They also had quite a chunk of meadow country up around Silver Lake, where the young stuff and replacement heifers were wintered. Back in those days, they never turned the bulls with the heifers until they were a full two years old or older.

They held more than two to three thousand replacement heifers each year. With weaners, yearlings, two year olds, and holdover steers, there were lots of cattle, and it took lots of country.

Christmas Valley, The Viewpoint, and a million nester ranches weren't there in those days. It was all big, wide, and open. I knew I'd found what I was wanting. So far as I was concerned, I landed in the right place.

That country up there, fenced in just two pastures, was where the replacement heifers were summered for seven or eight months. Actually there were three pastures if you counted the wrangle pasture which only had 14 sections.

Of the other two, one had 72 sections, and the other 73; a section being 640 acres, or a mile square.

A young fellow had to be about half wild and really crave the life, to hire out to one of those wagon crews; for you knew there wouldn't be anything but half broke snorty renegade horses to ride. And you were expected to do as much work, if not more, on "Ole Snorter," as the pensioners did on their half gentle horses. That term, "half gentle," is no joke either, for very few "cavvy" horses ever become truly gentle. Up there, they called the remuda, the "cavvy."

Out of a cavvy of 200 to 250 horses, there might be a half dozen that were gentle enough that you might let your sister ride if she was ranch raised and a pretty good hand with horses herself.

Every so often, when convenient, the cowboys turned their tired horses out and replaced them with fresh ones. The wagon boss had to know all those horses and their dispositions, so as to cut horses out to a new hand. The horse wrangler also had to know all those horses and be able to tell them apart, even in the dark of the morning. He'd know if he had them all, or which ones were hid out.

I was young and got promoted to the horse wrangler job. The wagon usually kept 75 to 100 horses for the working cavvy. We changed horses two or three times a day when possible, but out on that desert range, you were very apt to have to put in a full day on the horse you left on in the morning.

Those desert days are long from May through August; 16 to 18 hours is the rule, rather than the exception. It shore takes a big stout horse to pack you 18 hours working! It seemed like there were eight days in every week, and 18 to 24 hours in every day! Not much bed time between night dark and "first light" next morning.

Red   ZX RANCH

I fell in with a good crew. Years later, I found out that most of those old boys had left Texas, Arizona, Old Mexico, or Wyoming, just ahead of a sheriff, but they knew how to handle livestock. They'd learned under adverse conditions; moonlight drives and such!

Back in those days, if you could ride a cranky horse, the ZX had a job for you. The life was for me. The horses were cranky, the range was endless, and there was no reason to go to town for months on end. So far as I was concerned, I landed in the right place.

In the spring, usually around the middle of March, the wagon pulled out to the

desert with the first herd of 10 to 12 thousand cows. There would usually be around 35 bedroll cowboys with that first herd. Several cowboys were left with that first herd to get them spread out on that high desert. Later in the spring, when all the cows were turned out, there would only be 8 to 12 cowboys left with the wagon. Five falls in a row, I was with the wagon getting in to winter quarters the day before Thanksgiving.

One fall, I'd drawn second wagon detail, not as a jigger boss, but just as a hand. They hauled me and Travis Count to the Silver Lake Ranch where there were 40 or 50 saddle horses waiting for us. Our immediate job was to saddle a couple and trail the rest about

65 miles north and east across Christmas Valley and The Sinks, and on up to the Dominique Camp. After we left the Silver Lake Ranch corrals, we went through one gate on the whole ride. That was the drift fence between Lake and Deschutes Counties that the Civilian Conservation Corporation had built in the 30's. There were two or three buckoffs, and one night either a mountain lion or bear scared our cavvy, but they hit a drift fence corner that was stout enough to turn them back, and we got them under control.

We spent a night at the Silver Lake Ranch, and luckily, breakfast. When Dora Arney set a meal out for you, especially after being out with a "greasy sack" wagon for five or six weeks, it was a thing you'd remember. She was a whale of a cook! It took a day to trail our horses to Mamie Farnsworth's camp on the Klamath Indian Reservation. Mamie was quite a gal! She was full Klamath Indian, and somehow

she'd inherited control of a large section of land.

They kept a cowboy crew ahorseback the year around, but I never stayed there steady around, then. The only way you'd get any time off, was to quit; so you could spend some time in a beer joint and get some rest. I was 15 years old when I first went there. My driver's license said I was 16, but I'd had it for almost a year! I had convinced the clerk at the time they'd made a mistake on my birth certificate.

We'd been in the high country for two or three months without being in town; so that first night in town, maybe I drank too much beer. Anyhow, the next morning, I was so sick, I couldn't hold my head up, much less get up and catch a horse to go to work. I was 16 plus years old at the time, and this was my first trip to town with a crew, after a full season of work. Rich Bradbury, the boss, informed me to, "Either get up and go to work, or Get the

Hell out!" My choice. Either work or leave. I quit and I left! A poor excuse, but it suited me.

I said I never stayed there steady, but I never quit in a storm. I guess I made some kind of a record. In 15 years, I quit the ZX 13 times. The last hitch there, I stayed three years! A long time for a drifting cowboy.

Red and Tom Dark

New Handle

One particular day on the ZX, we were down in the Klamath Marsh, which the ZX Ranch had leased from the Klamath Indian Reservation in Oregon.

Late one afternoon, when the crew got in, the cookie said the "Candy Wagon" driver had brought some mail out from Paisley that morning. As he was reading off the names on the few letters, he came to mine. Red Wolverton. He tried to read it, but scrambled it up pretty well. For some reason, he just couldn't put Wolverton together.

"Who in the devil is this, with a name like that?" With an embarrassed grin, I stood up, with my hand out, and says, "That would probably be me."

Old Cookie says, "That's not your handle anymore! From now on, you're just plain **'Red Cloud!'** "

It stuck with me all my life. For years, all my mail came to me, simply as 'Red Cloud,' wherever I happened to be in 'Cow Country.'

48

A Cowboy's Outfit

A drifting cowboy don't need much, just a few necessary items: a good bedroll inside a good waterproof tarp 7' x 18'. If you only get to spend a few hours out of 36 in a bed, you need a good one. You need a pair of Blucher boots, Crockett spurs, and a Stetson hat. Of course a pure silk "wild rag" was essential! And Levis! And while we were there, I learned the difference between a 'California hotroll' and a genuine cowboy bedroll. A 'California hotroll!' is what was called those "fly by night" beds for inexperienced guys that came out to hire on a wagon crew. It didn't take them long to learn the facts of cowboy life.

You save up your money as you can, so as to be able to buy these until you have a good outfit. Of course, the expensive ones like a hand-carved Hamley saddle, and a bridle with a silver mounted Garcia bit take a while.

The ZX in pictures

Horseshoeing

I had to shoe horses for a while to have money to move on. Horseshoeing is an art which covers much territory; therefore it would require volumes of material to cover the field, even though roughly. Since I don't have time to give a complete report and do not feel qualified to analyze every type of horses to be shod; I shall mostly try to cover one angle of the horseshoeing of the cowpony. The equipment that a person needs is as follows:

- A shoeing rasp, (to file off the nails and rasp the hoof smooth after the shoe is put on)
- A pair of hoof nippers
- A pair of shoe pullers (in case the horse you are working on has old shoes which must be removed)
- A hoof knife to trim the frog and clean the bottom of the hoof
- A shoeing hammer
- A heavy hammer to shape the shoes with
- An assortment of horseshoe nails, ranging from size five to size six
- An assortment of "cowboy plates" (horseshoes), ranging from size double ott to size four
- A strong sacroiliac
- And a horse!

We shall assume here, that the horse which is to be worked on is gentle and that his feet may be picked up and worked on without any fuss. For here again, it would require another volume of words to describe all the means by which a cranky or hard to shoe horse, might be handled. Since we have started on the cowpony, we shall handle him as a cowboy would instead of using the blacksmith's method. Lead the horse to an open

place and hobble his forefeet; so that he will stand still. It is customary for a cowboy to shoe a horse's hind feet first, starting on the left side. That's where we shall start.

Stand approximately three feet in front of the horse's hind foot, facing at about a 45% angle towards the horse's rear. Place your left hand on the horse's left hip and run your right hand gently down his left leg. Gently grasp the leg by the fetlock and lift upwards and backwards. Place his leg over your left leg with his hoof resting between your knees. Trim the dead frog and dead sole from the hoof with the hoof knife, and then trim the

protruding shell of the hoof down as closely to the quick as possible. Trim the shell of the hoof close as possible also, and shape the shoe so that the shoe matches the quick, which is located just inside the shell, and is usually located from one quarter to one-half inch inside the shell of the hoof. Place the shoe and drive the nails in with the tops so that they protrude about three quarters of an inch up the side of the hoof. Twist the sharp points off with claws of the hammer. After all the nails are driven in, clinch them by holding a square piece of metal under the small end of the nail. Finish with clinches.

One time when I was shoeing, things went bad. When a big horse straightened out a front leg just as I drove a nail through the horseshoe, things turned out bad! That nail went into my finger under a ring I was wearing.

I had to hold his front end up with my right hand, while I pulled my left hand off the nail. If I hadn't, he would have squashed my hand and me into the ground under him.

As I recall, he jumped and kicked at me when I first let his front end down. It was no problem getting that ring off my bloody injured finger. It was a large gold plated ring with a large stone on the top. A beauty that had cost me more than I could afford at the time. I looked at that ring in my right hand, and says, "Adios!" as I threw it out in the timber as far as I could. I've never worn a ring since that day. Enough horseshoeing! It was time to drift some more.

The Smile of Fortune

Now I been lots of places
And seen lots of things.
Loved lots of women
And had lots of flings.

I've travelled this old world
For many a mile;
Had lots of troubles
And stood many a trial.

I once went to Reno.
I gambled and won.
And at playing the horses;
I was the favored one.

The smile of Fortune
Always shined upon me.
'Till I met a fair maiden
Who turned the tables easily.

Today I received your letter
It made me very lonesome and blue.
For I know I could never again
Find someone to take the place of you.

Maybe someday I'll meet
A girl, with Love True.
'Till then, I'll punch cattle
In the dust and the dew.

Elko Nevada

Elko was the main cow town for Nevada back in those days. I had an old map that claimed the entire population of the state was about 56,000 people then. I stopped in Elko one day, where I fooled around, looking the town over some, and had a drink or two in the Commercial Hotel and Gambling Parlor.

Inside I saw the biggest bear (stuffed), standing upright on its hind feet in a glass walled cage or enclosure. The sign gave the weight and height of the snow white polar bear. It seems like it weighed almost 1,400 pounds and stood about 13 feet tall. It was magnificent.

One of the next times I was in Elko several years later, there had been a bad fire which completely demolished the casino, and likewise burned up the polar bear. What a shame! It was a rarity which will probably never occur again.

That time, lo and behold, I ran into Harry Price, one of my old time cowboy friends. He was the ranch boss on Tom Tanner's ranch up on the North Fork. He was in town looking for some ranch hands. It was the start of haying season. He wanted me to come help run the haying and stacking crew. When he said they had four head of good large matched Belgian buck-rake horses that he needed someone like me to handle them; well, that convinced me. I spent the summer there.

In the fall, I was introduced to Tom's unmarried, pregnant sister-in-law. She was a good looking, pleasing sort of a gal, but when I figured out she needed a husband, and hinted that I might qualify, I decided it was time to move on.

So, back to being a 'Bedroll Cowboy' again. I left Nevada to see "What's over the next hill?" I spent the winter back on the ZX and another small ranch or two, and somehow, I wound my way to Vermejo Park, New Mexico.

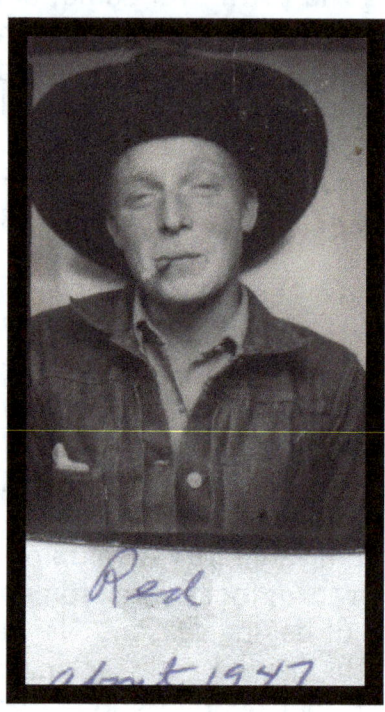

Red
about 1947

Vermejo Park

The WS Ranch ran about 11,000 mother cows at that time. The headquarters of the ranch was almost a town in itself. It had a large commissary, blacksmith shop, houses for married men, and a large cookhouse. I was hired to help do some cowboy work there. Several of my favorite yarns came out of that ranch.

Mules at Vermejo

I had the snappiest span of mules at my camp. They were only about 13 hands high, slim, and feisty. They were a jack and a jenny; buckskins with black rings on their legs, black manes and tails, and stripes down their backs. I used them on a two wheeled flat- bed cart sort of a wagon, to haul salt around to different locations there in the high country.

One day I had about a dozen blocks of salt I wanted to scatter out on a lower grade from my camp. I came out of a gate in the southwest corner of my wrangle pasture, at the top of a steep slope heading to the lower area.

I was working my way around this slope, which kept getting steeper to my left, as I went forward. Suddenly, the cart started sliding sideways, and I had to bail off on the high side. to save my neck or other parts. I tried to hang on to my mule lines, but they were jerked out of my hands as the cart took salt and mules sideways, then rolling over and jerking the mules down!

Finally, after a hundred feet or so, it all came to a stop. The empty cart by now, stopped right side up, with the mules still hooked to it. They were a little tangled up but I finally got them unhooked and untangled and hooked back up. I just left that salt scattered on that slope, thinking the cows would probably find it.

There was no way I could get back up over the slope to my camp; so I'd best mosey on down to the valley, where I knew there was a dirt entry road to the ranch, that I could follow it back up a couple miles to get back to my camp.

When I got in the valley, my mules were still ouchy from their drag off the slope, and they wanted to run; so I threw the slack to them and yelled something like, "Let's head for camp in a good lope!"

About that time a big limousine type of car in a cloud of dust saw us, and seemed like they hit their horn. Anyhow, it didn't take much to booger my mules. I guess they were trying to duck off to the side away from that contraption. I was standing up, beating and jerking on them, trying to keep them in the valley, instead of bolting up the side of the hill. I had about a foot of fiery red beard as I hadn't shaved all summer.

The yarn I got the next time the candy wagon driver came by my camp, was something like this: Those people in the limo had seen the wildest sight ever as they came down the valley road.

There was a team of mules running full blast in front of a big 2 wheeled cart, with a wild man with a long red beard blowing back over his shoulder, standing up and whipping the mules, trying to make them run faster!

New Mexico Gentrys

Out in remote Nevada, 50 miles from the nearest thing, I was sitting in a saloon one night. A cowboy looking feller, (not a buckaroo) like most of the Nevadans were at that time, came in and sat down at the opposite end of the bar. He kept looking my way and kept moving closer to where I was.

Finally, three or four stools away from me, he comes out with, "I don't mean no insult, but you don't look like a Nevada buckaroo." My reply was, "You look like one of those Las Vegas, New Mexico Gentrys to me." His eyes popped open, and he replied, "What makes you say something like that?"

"You look just like Bill Gentry," I replied.

"You knew him?"

"Sure, Bill and I traded about everything that two cowboys working together could trade. What you doing out here in Nevada?"

"Well, there was a rumor going around, that I'd been accused of some 'slick-earing' down in that area, and I figgered it was time to disappear for a while."

Said he'd been out on a remote ranch for about six months, and the first time he'd been back in civilization, he'd been recognized!

"Don't worry." I answered, just before buying him a drink. He started in, with something like this. "Now I know who you are. On a wall calendar in a line camp in the high country, I read one day, "Stayed in camp today because of a bad blizzard, September 13th, 1950. Red Cloud."

"Also, you remember that time down at headquarters, when you was the first in the round pole horse corral to catch your horse. As you were getting ready to rope, one of yours whirled, lunged, and jumped over your head. When he hit the ground, you had a loop around his left front ankle. You just coiled your slack, opened the gate, and led your horse out, with just the rope on his front ankle. He followed you like he had the rope around his neck!"

"I wasn't there that day, but it was talked about after that, all around the ranch."

"A while later, we were catching horses. You remember the old Mexican cowboy, Vargas?"

I nodded, "Yes."

"On this day, he'd spotted the horse he wanted. As he pitched his Houlihan out, his horse saw what was up, and switched ends in a jiffy, with his tail in the air. Vargas jerked his rope so as not to catch something else, but, Low and Behold! Where should that loop drop, but just around his horse's tail, where a crupper would be! He sees what he's got, and he says,

"Now if I was that damned Red Cloud, I'd just lead him out!" That brought out a good laugh from the crew.

I never saw that Gentry feller again, after that night.

I liked the country and that WS Ranch, and I should have stayed there, but things happen! I was told to come down to headquarters and bring three or four of my horses, to help do some cowboy work there. I hadn't had a sit down meal, other than what I fixed for myself, in several months. I was looking forward to a good headquarters' noon dinner.

When we came into the dining room, there was nothing on the table but about a dozen paper sack lunches. No food! It went on that way a few days. After I got back up to my camp, I decided, if you don't like the way an outfit is run, there's another outfit down the road a ways that does things different. A poor excuse, but enough for me to drift on again.

64

Happy Hobo

I've got a hole in my pocket;
Worn out shoes where I stand
Got no feather bed to sleep on;
Just sleep where I can.

Don't ask me where I'm going'
'Cause I don't even know.
They tell me I'm an outcast.
Just a plain old hobo.

One time I had a lot of money.
Had a wife and a home.
But a lot of greedy people
Wouldn't leave me alone.

Then my wife became a stranger
Not the girl I used to know.
I left her one day.
Now they call me a hobo.

There are times when I'm hungry.
There are times when I'm cold;
But my soul will never wear
The sign that says "Sold!"

For I can walk in dignity
No matter where I go.
I'm proud and I'm happy
Just to be a hobo.

Someday I'll meet my Maker,
And proudly I'll stand,
As He smiles I'll know

He'll reach and take me by the hand.

He'll say I've thoughts to tell you
And a lot of things to show,
You've finally reached your goal.
You Holy Heaven Hobo.

The Devil's Garden

I wound up near Alturas, California where I went to work to help gather the "Devil's Garden" country. This ranch ran in a big rough country. It was a good country to ride in, but had some drawbacks. It was an area about 50 or more miles north and south, with 20 or more miles east and west. It was flat rolling country with a lot of junipers and sagebrush.

The worst thing that you sure had to watch out for was there were many spring areas that did not run out of the ground, but came up to the surface, and were boggy in and around them. They had no bottom! But that was not why I finally drifted again.

Me and Leppy went to work for a young cowboy Andy that had got the cow boss's job because his dad and the owner were old time ranch friends. His father knew lots of cattlemen and had lots of pull in government circles.

Consequently, the boy that got the job as the boss of us three riders was the one with the least cow savvy which is usually about the way things go, but we didn't care a bit about that. I let him be boss occasionally, but at times, I just had to take the bossing job away from Andy, so as to get the work done.

I'm damned sure the 'Devil's Garden' wasn't misnamed! It was all malipais rock with sagebrush and juniper; rolling country with no landmarks to set your compass on. It was high desert, but it had springs that just popped up in the desert floor.

If you rode across one of those places, maybe just a few feet in diameter, a horse would drop like stepping in a hole. You'd flop off as best you could, and your horse would have a devil of a time getting back on solid ground. The only good thing was that those native horses were hard to ride into one of those places. It sure made you spooky to be trying to head an old cow and have one of those wet suck holes loom right up in front of you.

Ordinarily, the fall gathering there had been done by a crew of ten or eleven riders, mostly local men. Andy told the owner we could do it. We didn't need any extra help.

Andy, as boss that morning, told me to get our camp outfit together, enough for four or five days, but keep it as slim as possible. The three of us had thrown a 'greasy sack outfit' together. We moved our camp outfit up on one pack horse.

That first evening, when Andy went to make up some dough-gods, he asked where the mixing bowl was.

"You said, "Keep it slim. I didn't bring one," I replied.

"How we gonna mix up anything?" was his question.

I got the sack of flour out, opened up the top, and hollowed out the flour like a bowl. Into that flour bowl, I put baking powder, salt, and shortening. Then I added watered-down canned milk, and proceeded to stir it around until it was the right consistency to pinch the dough-gods out and fry them on the grill with the meat and taters. We cooked everything in the same skillet, and if we'd had company, I don't know what we'd fed them in. We just had what we needed.

Andy was the "boss," but every morning, while he was messing up the hotcakes, he would tell Leppy and me what the plans were for the day. We'd mull it over, and if it was nothing serious, we'd let Andy be the boss. We'd used quite a bit of patience, trying to teach him how to handle a trail herd, but we had trouble getting the fact across that the drags might follow the rest of the herd easily, if they weren't crowded too much. If it took a little extra past cow experience, more than we figured Andy had; Leppy and I would decide who'd be the Segundo that day.

Our first work was to ride the country for young barren cows to send to market. There was a set of corrals and a large lot on a lake at the upper end of the Garden. We decided we'd work that country first. We could hold our cows in the water lot, and when we got a hundred or so, trail them down to the big fenced-in meadow at the main camp. We'd hold them there until we got a large enough herd to trail them on down to the main ranch.

Andy was a good hand and a good guy, but like I said, he'd spent a lot of time in agricultural college, while Leppy and I were out tormenting the cows.

We weren't making a " working the herd" type of roundup and gather. We'd just start out, find a bunch of cattle, work them on the go; taking dry, barren cows with us on to the next bunch. We'd keep it up until we got all we could hold. If we got split up too much, then we'd head for camp where we had a pole corral and some baled hay. Every few days, we'd take what we'd gathered to a fenced in pasture, ten or twelve miles down the country.

This probably sounds like a "wild hare" way to gather cows, but the three of us "greasy sacking it," gathered more cows in less time than a nine man crew had ever done it before.

We each had a full string of horses though, and it was a good thing we did. That Devil's Garden country is some rough, and it's a big country. Also the cattle weren't exactly milk pasture type!

One morning about daylight, we decided it was time to move our gather to the lower country again. It was one of those cold, rainy, half foggy mornings, common to the high desert country, that just about freeze you to death; and that cause even your gentlest horses to have a hump in their back when you saddle up.

This morning was one of the worst. After lying for a few hours in the rain in a wet bed; then trying to burn some flannel cakes over a smoky fire in the pitch dark; well, there just weren't any words wasted that morning on socializing.

I was the first to the corral, and I had just undone my lass' rope. I stepped into the horse corral, when all of a sudden: Whoosh!

Our cattle jumped up from where they were lying down, or standing in the next corral; and in a run as hard as they could go in a mass, they hit the far side of the corral! There was a sickening, splintering of our corral poles. There the whole herd of several days of hard riding was flying to freedom as fast as they could go!

There was about a half mile of fairly flat open country between the busted corral and a solid wall of junipers. Once they reached the timber, it would be almost impossible to catch any sizeable bunch of them before they scattered and got clean away.

That's what I was thinking as I ran across the corral, shaking out a loop and snaring it on the first one of my string that got in range.

I'd bet, if that old hoss could talk, he'd say it was the fastest job of saddling he'd ever witnessed in his life. I jerked the bridle on, grabbed my saddle from under my blankets and slung it over his back.

As the cinch swung under his belly, I run the latigo through it and jerked the loose end up. With a swing and lunge, I landed in his middle, whooping and whipping and spurring!

The coils of my lass' rope were over my left arm, with the loop still around his neck. The reins were in my left hand, both on the same side of his neck.

The first hundred yards were the worst. For a while, I didn't think I was going to make it. The herd of cattle were still staying together, but were eating up the distance to safety. My old Hamley was really slopping. Every jump felt like we were going to go overboard, right over his withers, but I didn't have time for foolishness or concern; so after awhile, my old hoss quit his bucking and stampeded in the right direction too, but it didn't even slow them down.

It was between a quarter and a half mile to heavy timber. They were in a bunch. If I could beat them to the timber, maybe I could turn them. If not, they'd be Hell to gather again.

I out ran the cows and came in just right to haze them away from the timber and toward open country. Just before the lead cows made it to freedom, I steamed up on the near point, and was able to bend them. The whole herd followed right on out to open county, where I had the cows milling and pretty well quieted down by the time Andy and Leppy showed up.

Of course, Andy and Leppy weren't moseying along. They got saddled about as fast as I did and came to my rescue. I had just got a good head start on them.

We were headed in the right direction and were a couple miles on our way before we got the cattle settled down some and lined out for the lower country, I left the other two boys to go back to camp for my saddle blankets. As I turned to ride away, Andy mentioned, "You just as well bring the 30-30. We might see a good antelope, and we're pretty low on camp meat."

Packing a rifle didn't amount to much to my old hoss, after what he'd been through already this morning, so we were back to the trail in short order. About noon, Andy spotted some antelope over a rise; so I gave him the rifle and took his horse while he slipped out and shot one.

I guess you know who got elected to pack it back to camp, but I didn't mind as I was looking forward to getting some of it in a skillet right away. We finally wound up blind-folding and hobbling my horse to get the antelope up behind my saddle. After we got it anchored good, I took the hobbles off, then planted myself in the riggin'. I finally reached down and slipped the blind-fold from my old snorter.

It was comical the way that old pony carried on each time he'd look around and see that antelope. Down would go his head, and he'd buck and bawl, and try to run out from under it; but I reckon we had it latched on pretty good, because everything was still right in place when we got to camp.

Fresh antelope steak is pretty good out in a greasy sack camp, when you haven't got much of anything else to eat. Those other boys thought so too, that evening after spending 14 hours between meals.

While we were on the beef gather, we picked up several head of four, five, or six year old steers that belonged to another ranch. These old boys were a little bit snorty. It took some high riding, ripped clothes and torn bruised skin, to get them gathered in.

We figured we couldn't draw any extra wage for the stray cattle we'd gathered; so we decided to collect our pay right out of that herd, by team roping all the strays! We spent a most enjoyable day until us and our horses were give out, from playing with the neighbors' cattle.

After we finally got through with the beef gather, and had everything moved down to our fenced pasture at our main camp; we rode out one morning and bunched the herd to check for stray brands; so we could notify all the rightful owners to come claim their cattle.

We had about 500 head in the half- section trap, along with the strays of several local ranchers. We notified everybody concerned that we'd hold a "rodera" and they could come and cut out their strays.

We finally got the word out to all the owners of the stray cattle, and made a date for the day they would come get them.

That day, the six or eight different neighbors showed up, we rode out and threw a roundup together, out in the middle of the meadow. Each neighbor took his turn getting his strays, until it finally came time for the old boy that owned the big renegade steers.

He had on a pair of old overalls, and had a work horse bridle on his horse. As it was his turn, he rode up closer to the roundup. That old rancher had five big, three- or four- year- old steers that had dodged the gathering for two years.

Stopping, he started calling his steers, but they didn't come out of the herd. They just stood, shaking their heads and looked at him.

"Sook, Boys, Sook Boys, Here Boys!"

It was plain to see his old renegade steers knew him, for when he started calling, they all turned and faced him; some even came part way across the roundup toward him. A couple even bawled gently in answer to him.

After trying several times more with his "Sook Boys," to no avail, he really set us to snickering. I can still hear that old man saying, when he came out with, "What's the matter, Boys, has these fellers been chousing you and got you all wild?"

We'd choused them some alright, the wild-running sons of guns, but we figured we'd done the old man a favor. Some of those steers had wintered out for two or three years or longer. When we finally got them out in the open country, we team roped them all just for the Hell of it. We finally had to work them out for the old man, and help him away with them.

The three of us started that herd to the headquarters ranch. We had fat dry cows and about 150 old cows with calves in the herd

We were supposed to get some help from headquarters ranch to help us through town. Here we were within a quarter of a mile from town, and not a soul had shown up. Leppy and I were riding point and swing, crossing back and forth across the trail to keep cattle in line.

The first couple days, we let Andy be boss until about the middle of the morning. I decided I better ride to where I could see how Andy was doing. It seemed there were more and more cows in the trail all the while, without a calf.

I rode back from the lead. Sure enough, there was Andy, riding back and forth behind about 100 calves and about a dozen cows, yowling his head off and rattling a large tin can with rocks in it.

I sat up there for a little while watching the commotion, trying to decide what I was going to do. I could see that as soon as we got into town and at the first scare, all those calves would stampede back to our last night's bed ground. I knew there were a number of nesters just waiting for us high-powered imported cowboys to lose a herd, so they could come to our rescue. They'd talk about how these cowboys had tried to show the old timers how the hog ate the cabbage; but then the old Home Guard had to be called out, when it came to some really serious cow handling.

Our main problem at the present was to get the calves mothered up, and quick, before they turned and ran right over us, going back down the trail.

I knew what Andy was thinking too, as he looked up several times, in the short while I sat there,; wondering why I didn't come down and help him crowd that army of calves up into the herd. That's just not the way things are done.

I finally realized I just couldn't ride away from a trail herd just because I didn't like the way things were going, but I decided I could run a 'sandy' on Andy; so I hit a lope down to where Andy was.

He met me with some silly remark about how were we going to crowd these calves up into the herd. I really felt like a heel, but I had to take drastic steps to get that herd straightened out, and to protect all our reputations. After all, Andy had hired us; so I had to prove to the outsiders that he knew what he was doing, to make hiring us a smart move.

"Andy," says I, "I'm going to give you a choice: either you turn the bossing of this herd over to me now, and you do just what I say to do, or else I'll just turn and ride off to camp, and you can do whatever you please."

I really felt sorry for Andy. He thought he was doing such a good job, and here I'd just dealt him one right off the bottom. He just looked down at his horse's ears for a time with a blank look before he ups and grins, kind of half- heartedly at me and says, "OK Boss, How will we handle it?"

I told Andy to quit pushing the calves and to see if he could just hold them. "Just stay behind the drags, don't crowd them, but be real careful not to let a calf turn back on him."

If one calf would have turned back, and got a start, the whole bunch would have doubled back like a swarm of bees.

Right then our herd was strung out for about a half mile, sort of going around the left side of a knoll. Our lead cows were mothered up and feeling good and wanting to travel; so we just couldn't stop them and hold them 'till the drags caught up. We didn't have enough men to double right back on the same trail. The only answer was to keep the leaders on the move but bend them around in a circle and bring them right back up through the drags.

I hit a high lope up the left of the trail. Leppy knew what we'd do as soon as I told him I'd traded Andy out of his bossing job.

I was going to circle the lead around that knoll off to the right and bring them around and back up through the calves. Then when we started out again, he and Leppy were going to stay with the lead. He was going to stay away from the drags, and we'd go on.

We were real lucky. Our lead gave right to our slight pressure and headed right around the knoll. With Leppy on the point, I dropped back on the swing and about the time I could see the lead coming up behind the drags, the ratio of calves to cows in the trail began to drop, so the trail was easy to chop off; and those lonesome cows were glad to go back hunting for their calves.

The three of us were plenty able to hold the cattle then in a loose herd while the cows and calves paired up again. It worked better than I'd hoped it would, and almost every calf mothered up and went on with its mammy. I just let the drag mostly take care of themselves.

As soon as I was satisfied with the lead, I'd come back and take over the rear of the herd, and he'd come ride point across from Leppy. In less than half an hour, we had everything paired up and were ready to move out, again.

Andy's orders were to stay on the backside of the herd, while Leppy and I got the herd started on toward town. Going into a bad place, the lead men have to be right there in the exact place at the exact time to keep the point aiming ahead. Just one slip and the point starts milling; then you really got problems.

Andy and Leppy, once we got into the residential area, were to stay right with the point. Keep it moving in the right direction, and keep the lead cows from breaking into a run or going too fast.

We'd got the herd moving well, and I'd traded places with Andy. Things were shaping up real good. There were only four or five extra calves in the drag; actually there wasn't any drag. The herd was about the same size all the way, for the half mile or so we had it strung out, by the time we reached town.

Here, we had some more luck. An old Indian on a stove up horse, showed up to help us; so I had him follow the drag which left me free to watch the swings. Luckily, I was pretty far ahead toward the point, as it came to a dry cleaning establishment. Just as the point was even with the place, the pop off valve on a steam boiler joined the party with a big huff of steam 15 feet high and half way across the street!

Before the air had cleared, I was in a dead run up that blacktop street on a slick-shod horse. Like a covey of quail, the point busted to the left for places unknown, and a big vacant lot. The three of us all got in position about the same time. Busy we were, trying to hold the point together, and keep it out of a mill, while at the same time, keep it moving in some semblance of a forward direction, while trying to hold it down out of a run.

It took us a block or two, to bring the point down to a slow trot. Old Lady Luck was with us again. The spark of fear had flown the whole length of our herd, and when our lead broke into a gallop, the whole herd speeded up forward. By the time we got them slowed down to a trot, the drags had pulled up to within about a quarter mile behind us.

And sure enough, there bounding along behind us was the old Indian. We decided right quick, that our best bet was to hold that trot right on through town.

It was kind of comical, as we busted right out on Main Street, among traffic and pedestrians for that last short block, before we could cross the bridge out of town. 450 cows with big calves by their sides isn't any great big herd, but it's a mass piling down a street at a good trot in close formation!

The help at headquarters was just getting ready to come help us through town, when we trailed into their ranch. It was only about 7:30 A.M., and we'd had a total distance of five or six miles to come that morning. The "home guard" boys weren't used to rolling out quite as early as we were.

We made it to the meadow where all the cattle were left together for a few days to rest. We drank a little beer that night before starting out on a hog roundup the next day.

I didn't know what we were up to, but should have figured something was up when Andy and Leppy both caught young horses, and Andy casually suggested I ride my good roping horse.

A lot of the ranches used to run hogs semi-wild. They'd just let them run in the meadows and gather them like cattle when they needed a fresh supply of pork.

Well, Andy informs us we were going on a hog roundup. We'd corral them in a big high boarded-to-the-ground corral. When we finally got them all corralled, Andy informed me that he and Leppy would do the ground work; castrating, ringing, and so on, on the 40 to 50 pound pigs.

All I had to do was ride into the hog corral and catch the young pigs and drag them out. The hog corral was full of sows, boars, and young pigs, all mixed together. Andy and Leppy would run the gate to keep the sows in when I drug a pig out at a hard lope. They'd "flat-ass" the pig like a calf and do the work, then turn the pig back inside when finished.

There were several sows and a couple boars that stood as high as my stirrups ahorseback. They all had tusks shining at me.

A couple times, the boys didn't get the gate shut in time to cut the sow off, so I'd have to make a circle, ride back into the hog corral while dragging the pig, and then escape those long snapping tusks, while circling back to ride outside again. Of course all this time, those pigs are squealing as only pigs know how to do.

We finally got them all worked without any serious mishaps, but if you really crave a thrill, you should try that sometime.

When we went back to The Devil's Garden to finish our fall work, Andy mentioned to the owner that we were sort of short on horses.

All the owner said was, "There's lots of young horses out there. Use them."

We gathered a bunch of 15 or so into our wrangle trap. When we came in that evening, if it wasn't full dark; we'd catch a couple, get a hackamore on them, and tie them up for the night. We had a good stout corral for this. They didn't have too much

buck in them the next morning when we went to use them.

One day Andy and Leppy were both riding broncs, and I was on a good cow horse. Now, like lots of semi-desert country, some of that open country was so big it took three looks to see clear across it to the distant horizon or low hills.

I don't remember why, but Leppy went off on a circle, planning to meet us over yonder sometime around noon. He was in camp when we finally got in.

One of my great desires was to rope an antelope. I knew it could be done. If I'd just keep my eyes open and watch, I'd get the opportunity.

One bright crisp fall day, we were gathering cows and I got my chance to rope my antelope., but all sorts of disaster struck!

We'd been riding quite a while together. It was a big country and you could see for miles in most every direction. We'd finally got a little herd gathered up when Andy decided that Leppy could follow them on down country, the way we were going, and that he and I would make a big circle out to the left around a pretty good sized lake.

We'd ridden out several miles and finally had a little bunch of cows, and were working down toward where we were to come together with Leppy. We were moseying along with them, when we spotted a band of 40 or 50 antelope out on a narrow piece of land that ran way out in the lake.

We were travelling sort of parallel to the lake, about a half mile and over a low ridge from it. I was riding off to the side of our herd, along the ridge, to where I could see down to the lake. Pretty soon, I spied what I'd been looking for, a point of land running out into the lake and, out on the point, a band of antelope. We'd both always wanted to rope an antelope

Well, I drops back over the ridge and heats Andy up, with the fact that one of us is sure going to get his rope on an antelope!

We decided we'd ride right down the center of the finger of land toward the band. Then when they saw us, they'd break for open country between us, and the water, on one side or the other.

Andy wasn't too anxious to get his rope in motion, as he was riding a bronc on his first ride in the open country, but he got his loop shook out somehow, and I had a loop poked in the business end of mine. We got between the antelope and the free country before they saw us, and there they came right on close by us.

They can outrun a horse for a ways, and we were letting them drift by. A real good young buck was coming up in range of my rope. We were running full out, and I was just ready to sail my loop, when I felt my horse hit a very odd gait. He was running on only one front leg. A three inch strip of hide was all that was holding his hoof to his body.

We got stopped without a fall, and there was nothing I could do. It was ten miles across roadless rocky desert back to our camp. I had to put my good horse out of his misery, a very hard thing to do.

There we were. Two men, two heavy stock saddles, and one bronc horse.

"What do we do now?" asked Andy.
I 'surpogulated' the situation over for a spell and then came out with, "Go run those cows back over this way. Catch me a good stout one, and I'll saddle her and ride her home."

It was just a short ways to where the cows were, so I figured he'd be right back. After a half hour or so, I got worried and hoofed it to the highest piece of ground around. Off in the near distance grazed our cows, but no Andy. I was getting worried but then noticed that, off to my left was a band of horses, Andy hot behind them, leaving a dust cloud behind as they headed directly my way.

I had my lass' rope, so I ran back to my saddle and got my long yellow slicker. The horses were coming on my side of the lake.

I got behind a juniper bush, and, at the right time, I jumped out flagging the slicker, and was able to turn them right down the peninsula where we'd run the antelope. Andy ahorseback and me a-foot, built right in behind them and ran them off into the lake.

"Catch me a good one when they come out," I yelled, as I started throwing rocks at them to keep them going.

When they came out, Andy was right in the middle of them, and he latched onto a big fat stout, strawberry roan mare. This was the first time his old pony had seen anything like that. Actually, it was his first ride outside a corral!

Andy took his turns, and his horse blew the plug. He was doing a good job of it too. The old roan mare sold out and ran the other side of a 20 foot tall juniper tree. That tree really gave both horses a whale of a jerk!

Of course, all this time, I was coming full bore as fast as old Shank's pony could get me there.

I cast a loop about the time the mare's front feet were coming back to earth, and picked them both up. There was a good snag stump there, and I was able to get my turns on it with my rope, and we got the mare down.

Andy's horse had quit bucking when his rope came tight around the juniper.

I ran up and got the mare's feet tied together so she couldn't get up. Then we rolled her some and I got my cinch underneath and my saddle on her back. I took the chin strap off my grazer bit, the better to pull her head around without a curb strap.

We got the ropes off her feet, and I came up with her. We boiled up a little desert, but then I got her lined out and rode back to camp. I don't know why I didn't keep her and use her the rest of the fall, except that back in those days, a good ranch cowboy wouldn't be caught dead riding a "Nelly!"

The Devil's Garden was a good piece of country for a drifting cowboy. It had drawbacks like most good things do. It had dangerous spots like small quicksand spring holes that were hard to see on a running horse if you were new to the area. It had wild cattle that hid out, and mountains all around it miles away that were hard to spot from the juniper covered lowlands. It was easy to get lost in but it was still a cowboy's preference.

I think Zane Grey's yarn about Forlorn River was written when he was at the headquarters of the Devil's Garden Ranch a long time ago.

I would have probably stayed there longer but Andy thought he was the only one that knew how to cook breakfast. That was OK. But he thought we should have pancakes seven days a week, week in and week out. That would have still been OK, but the way he cooked them finally got to me.

He would put the batter on a grill that was too hot. Burn one side, then turn them over and burn the other side. Then he hollered. "Chuck." His cakes were burnt on both sides, but runny and doughy on the inside. To this day, if I order hotcakes, they have to be cooked all the way through, and preferably not burned black on both sides!

A poor excuse, but I think that was the reason for drifting again, when I left there.

Laughing Cowboys

As I remember, we were returning
From trailing a herd over the Rim.
When my bronco blew up and tried
To unseat that fellow called Slim.

He swallowed his tail in one wild leap,
And down the canyon we did fly.
I was a-pulling in slack,
And ducking for limbs to go by.

He would have bucked me off sooner,
In my mind, there is no doubt.
But just as I'd start to fall,
A limb would set me up straight as a jackpine sprout.

He packed me to an opening,
And there in a pile he left me for sure.
Trying so hard to get to my feet,
Was how I seen this laughing cowboy all in a blur.

Will that bronco ride double?
I mean do you think he will pack you and me?
If you want, we'll give him a try,
And if you have to walk, you'll have company.

Well, I eased up behind him
With all the skill I ever did know;
But that wasn't near enough
And I'm thinking it was a might too slow.

About three jumps was all I stayed,
Then turned a flip and hit the dirt.
Just a-laughing 'till I hardly could stand,
Cause I still had a handful of this cowboy' shirt.

Arm in arm, a-laughing,
We started, no worries, no cares, just then;
Just a couple wild young cowboys,
A-waiting our chance to do it again.

A Tough Break

When I was working as a cowboy on a large cow outfit in the northwest, my ambitions were similar to many of the young fellows of the time. I wanted to be a saddlebronc rider; but where they were mostly getting their experience in the rodeos, I had decided I would ride the broncs out in the sagebrush country until I was really good, before I spent any money on entrance fees to exhibit to the public what a cowboy I thought I was.

I asked for a gentle string of horses when I came to the ranch, for the reputation of their horses was that even the gentle ones all knew how, and would buck if they had half a chance.

I don't recall how many times I got bucked off that first fall. The falls and hard knocks were just a tempering to life in the open, ahorseback.

Finally I turned a couple of my gentler horses in and asked for two of the rough string ponies that I had seen buck, and that I figured I could ride. I made out pretty good for a while. I stole a few rides; that is, I got by without my horse bucking. Then I earned a few. I recall that a sorrel horse bucked fifteen times one day, and I was pretty near give out when we got back to the wagon that afternoon. The horse couldn't buck very hard, but when he'd start, he'd just keep going until he'd come to a fence or a ditch or something he didn't like the looks of, then he'd usually throw his head up and quit for a while.

The other horse, a black, wasn't nearly as large as the sorrel, but he had a lot more intelligence. He could buck a lot harder than the sorrel too, but most of the time he'd just buck a few jumps and then run off. He had injured two other cowboys that year in that manner; bucking a few jumps and then running off into the timber or someplace where he had the advantage over his rider. All in all though, I was getting lots of good practice toward my bronc riding career, and the thrills were there to be had.

It's much easier for a fellow to look back and see his mistakes than it is to look ahead and avoid them, especially when a horse is bucking. The decisions must be made and carried out in something less than an instant; and that was about all the time I had to decide what to do when this black horse blew up with me. We were in the timber, and, of course, he followed his old pattern of bucking a few jumps and then stampeding right through the thick trees. Mostly I was still with him when we cleared the first tree, that is; there was part of my clothes and lots of exposed skin missing, but I still had the old horse between my knees; and he was still making his long running bucks, heading for the next jackpine thicket. I never knew exactly what went wrong then, but I remember that when I looked up and saw that thicket coming toward me, that I decided something had to be done, and pronto!

I knew of one sure way to stop his stampeding, but it had its drawbacks too. When he was spurred in the shoulders hard enough, he'd quit his running and get down to serious bucking; which he could and would do in a very small area.

I must have got a little over ambitious with my spurring, for I always figured I hit the nerves to his front legs when I reached up and drove the steel to his shoulders, because he made one real high jump and came right straight down all the way, just sort of folding up and squashing together as he came back to earth.

I don't think I was knocked unconscious, but I was dazed, for the next thing I knew, I was standing up watching him tear off through the timber.

A few seconds later, a fellow on another rough string horse caught up with me. He'd been with me when it all started. "What'll we do now?" says he.

"Will that nag ride double?" I asked sheepishly.

"Well, if he won't we'll have each other's company walking home." He answered with a grin.

He bucked us both off in less time than it takes to tell about it. Since both horses had headed for camp, there wasn't much we could do but tag them in. It was only about eight miles.

Right away I began to notice I was having trouble walking, but I didn't say anything to this other boy. When we came out into a clearing after about half a mile, and saw the rest of the crew sitting, holding our horses, it was a welcome sight. It seems that they had seen us coming down off the mountain a while before and had decided to wait; and then when our ponies came running out of the timber, they were right on the spot.

The jog home (to the wagon) was pretty painful, but I made it and got my horse unsaddled. When I stooped over to get my bedroll, to take it and roll it out, I couldn't straighten up. One of the boys rolled my bed out and helped me in it, and there I spent a very long night.

I stayed around camp the next morning. Finally about four o'clock that afternoon, we all decided I should go to see a doctor.

We were in Sycan Marsh. It was rough mountain country and was only about 125 miles to Lakeview. The only transportation at that time was two rough-riding pickups. One of the other boys drove me to the hospital. It was quite a three to four hour rough ride.

They took me right in and put me to bed. They put me in traction. I spent two weeks with two 15 pound weights tied to my ankles, holding them down over the end of the bed, and a neck brace of some kind holding my head at the upper end of the bed.

After that, the doctor said he'd done all he could do for me, and turned me out and loose.
Hobbling down the street, I came by a chiropractor's sign. I'd never been to one before this, but decided to see if he could do anything for me. He checked and massaged me. He said it appears I had broken part of a vertebrae. Maybe massaging and adjusting my spine might let it heal up.

For the next two or three months, every time I'd make a misstep , it would pop out and I'd have to go back to Dr. Franklin. He finally told me it looked like the only way to get it fixed was with a spinal fusion.

After some other doctors in Klamath Falls said I should go to Portland where there were some spinal specialists; that's where I went. That was in October. After spending the rest of the winter in and out of a little desert town hospital, with undetermined back injuries, I finally got sent to Portland, Oregon, to some specialists in February. They decided I'd have to have a spinal fusion to get straightened up so I spent the next several weeks in four hour shifts. I would have to lie in one position for four hours, and then if I could persuade the nurses to turn me, I would put in another four hours in a new pose.

There were three positions; my stomach or either side. I had to get the nurses to turn me because almost all the movement a spinal fusion patient can manage, or is allowed, is the use of his hands and arms. Of course his brain is active. It just goes around and around in circles, day and night, asleep or wake. The worst part is that with all the pain and stress of the operation, it is too easy to become more concerned with oneself than anything else. Pretty soon you get to feeling sorry for yourself, and to thinking that maybe the doctors made some slight mistake in the operation, such as cutting into the nerves and that maybe you'll never be able to walk again, or at least handle your legs properly. Thoughts like that are pretty hard on a young fellow who is used to the wild free life of a cowboy!

I was lucky to get a short body cast which ran from my hip joints to my arm pits. Some are much larger, but even then, after I was able to get out of bed, it took the nurses several days to teach me to walk again.

Finally on a bright sunny April day, the doctors told me I could leave the hospital, but the world seemed pretty gray to me as I walked down the street. All I could think of was having to wear the body cast for the next three and a half months or so, then spending several more months of progressive exercise before I could return to my horses and my work. Even then, maybe I'd have to quit cowboying for a less strenuous job.

Then as I came up to a corner and stopped, a man's cheerful voice broke through my little shell.

"Would you mind helping me across the street, sir?" he asked.

Right then and there, my self-pity vanished; my dark clouds disappeared, and suddenly the world was a bright and cheerful place to me. I realized that when you get to feeling sorry for yourself, just look around. There is always someone in worse shape. For the man who had spoken to me with such a cheerful voice was in a wheel chair; and there I was, stepping right on across the street all on my own!

A Strong Corral

I used to run horses;
Tried to catch the wildest one.
To get my loop on an outlaw,
Was what I thought most fun!

I used to stand and watch them,
When they were in a strong corral;
With that heart-broken look they had,
They'd lost their freedom they loved so well.

They didn't bother me then,
As I didn't know how much freedom meant.
I didn't know how much they suffered,
Or through the misery they went.

With sympathy now, I understand
How their poor hearts did ache.
As I've been pinned up all winter,
And it's awful hard to take.

I look through the hospital window
And long for the distant purple hills;
Like a wild roving mustang
That longs for Freedom's thrills.

I know there is one thing
I could never stand so well,
To see a freedom loving
 mustang
Cornered in a strong corral.

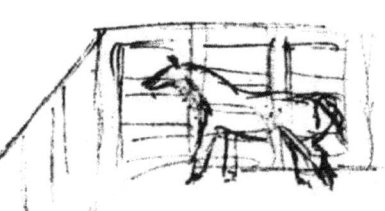

Wrap and Tangle

I started out roping as a "Tied hard and fast" man, but after I saw a fellow rope a bull, tied fast, and the bull charged him, I saw the predicament he was in. Recalling the same kind of an incident on a "wrap and tangle" outfit, where the rider coiled his slack and was able to handle it and maneuver his rope so much more efficiently, I decided the next outfit I worked for would be a dally outfit, so I could see and learn, and become a good dally hand after a while.

I went to work on an Irish outfit where all the hands were twice my age, and some had ropes twice as long as my 60 foot nylon. Theirs were all rawhide riatas, and the short ones were almost 85 feet long. They rode centerfire single rig saddles.

The only reason I went to work for that outfit was, well, I was out of a job and broke, as I was trying to heal up a broken leg, and I knew the rancher from some past doings. None of his crew would visit with me, when they saw my grazer bit, double rigged saddle, and short 60 foot nylon rope.

I'll say one thing for those old buckaroos. They did everything ahorseback. We gathered a big country, but to cut a long story short, when we got to headquarters I was put on the outside of the working corrals. There was a large round coral with smaller corrals off it, and one open alley that didn't have a gate. They put me in that open alley, probably to get me out of their way, but supposedly to see if I could turn back anything that got by them, and came that way, maybe I might be able to head it back to the corrals.

Well, one, a yearling heifer, 350 pounds or large that got by the buckaroos, came running just right for me to jump my horse ahead and turn her right back into where she came from.

Things don't always go according to plans. Now I've never been what I consider a good, consistent roper. I've made a few fabulous catches in my time, but I never could do it repeatedly.

I had my rope down, and a loop made. As I jumped my horse ahead to turn her, he fell flat on his front end! The heifer ducked behind me. As my horse was getting up, with the heifer behind me, I turned and twisted around. I throwed my rope behind me, over my left shoulder, and caught that heifer right around the neck, about 40 feet behind me. I took my dallies as my horse was getting up. I drug her back into the "rodera," and one of the Irish boys heeled her and got my rope off her neck.

No one said a word about what had just happened, but that night in the bunkhouse, they all spoke friendly toward me.

Jack and Casper

Most years, after the Lakeview Labor Day celebration, the ZX would put in a second wagon to gather the high desert and Klamath Marsh Indian country. One fall, I'd drawed second wagon detail, not as a jigger boss, but just as a hand. They hauled me and Travis Count to the Silver Lake Ranch where there were 40 or 50 saddle horses waiting for us. Our immediate job was to saddle a couple and trail the rest about 65 miles north and east, across Christmas Valley and the Sinks, and on up to the Dominique Camp. After we left the Silver Lake Ranch corrals, we went through one gate on the whole ride. That was the drift fence between Lake and Deschutes Counties, that the Civilian Conservation Corp had built in the '30's.

That country up there, fenced in just two pastures, was where the replacement heifers were summered for seven or eight months. Actually there were three pastures if you counted the wrangle pasture which had only 14 sections. Of the other two, one had 72 sections and the other 73; a section being a mile square or 640 acres.

We lucked out as we didn't have to pack our beds or shoeing outfits. The "Candy Wagon" took them for us. That was what they called the vehicle that hauled grub and supplies to the line camps. Hank McCall was the candy wagon diver. Good ol' Hank ran it and tended the windmills on the desert part of the ranch.

Slinghead Bown was our wagon boss. When you followed him on a roundup, you put in many miles a day. We had lots of good fresh horses when we started, so we really got with it. We gathered all that high desert and trailed the cattle to Silver Lake without a serious mishap.

There were two or three buckoffs, and one night, either a mountain lion or bear scared our cavvy, but they hit a drift fence corner that was stout enough to turn them back, and we got them under control.

We gathered all that country, trailed the cattle to Riley Crossing, and sent a whole trainload of cattle to California. The roundup with the second wagon was all caught up when we got back to Silver Lake, so me and another younger feller rode into Sycan Marsh. We joined the main wagon to help move cattle up through Currier Camp and over the Rim, where we turned them loose. From there, with the help of camp riders below, they'd drift past the Chalk Hills and on toward the Red House and the Chewaucan Marsh.

We didn't take any extra horses with us. We still had part of a string with the extra resting remuda in Sycan. The wagon was heading for Currier Camp the next morning and didn't have time to bring the extra horses. There were some spares in the remuda, so we were cut out a couple of them. I don't remember the horse I rode the first day. I think he was an "old man's horse," but we got the job done without putting on any exhibitions.

There were two new men I didn't know. Rough string bronc riders that had hired on while I was out with the second wagon. They were Casper Gunderson and Jack Carson, two cowboys just about as wild and wooly as they come. The next day, Lopey cut me a big old gentle bay horse that resembled a farm horse more than a cowhorse. Those boys got a lot of snickers when they observed me.

If things went just right, such as no blizzard and snow not too deep, and cattle moving right out, we could have the drags of the herd over the rim and turned loose heading downhill by noon or shortly thereafter. Then the procedure was to hurry back to the Currier Camp to the wagon, eat a quick bite, and turn back to Sycan Ranch by evening.

There was a foot or more of snow for the last couple miles before we reached the rim. By noon, the sun turned through real warm, and the downhill trail back to Currier was some slick and muddy.

The crew was strung out as some of them had headed back earlier. When we started back down that trail, joggin' along, Jack and Casper were a ways behind me. I noticed over my shoulder that they were getting their heads together for some kind of devilment. Apparently, they knew my old Rex horse better than I did. I'm sure they figured I was more of a gunsel than what I was, drawing a horse like Rex. I found out soon that if some riders were to gallop past him when you were heading for camp, he'd cold jaw and stampede. All you could do was yank on him and hope you made it back to camp.

I was keeping an eye on that pair behind me and saw them when they broke into a hard run. I had my lass' rope coiled, but just hanging over my saddle horn. I decided three could play. By the time they passed me, I had a loop built. I didn't try to rope them. I just kept them ahead of me. We were running too fast downhill on that muddy, slick ground for them to turn off.

I saw I couldn't pull Rex up, so any time either of them tried to pull up or slow down, I'd burn their horses' rumps with my rope. I just kept them ahead of me at full bore speed for a mile or more. They kept looking back trying to tell me to let up and they'd be good. I kept them ahead a long ways before I let them pull up as I shot between them.

I couldn't pull Rex up or slow him down. I finally got one rein in each hand. I was using a grazer bit, and I got to pulling on first one rein and then the other. He'd swing his head way out to either side. I saw a big pine tree, about three feet thick, up ahead of me in the trail. Rex had got to where he'd swerve a little to whichever side I pulled on. As the tree zoomed in closer to us, I pulled his head to the

outside away from the trail, then yanked it back to the tree side at the last instant. He swerved just enough that we were perfectly lined up with the tree before he saw it.

Rex jerked his head up enough that his nose went up the trunk. He must have tried to stop, but his four legs went around the tree, a front and hind leg on each side, as we slammed into it. I was clear up on his neck and got a pretty good jolt myself against the tree. It didn't break his fool neck, or knock his knot head in, but I think it sure knocked the wind out of him.

Somehow, we got back away from the tree, and I wallered back in my saddle. We sat there a minute or two getting our breaths, until I finally nudged him. I reined him back toward the trail and we jogged on into Currier. I might say we were quite a little ways ahead of Jack and Casper.

It was all in a day's pranks, and Casper and Jack and I became good pals after that, working together the rest of the winter.

104

Lonesome Cowboy

After you have lived
A Life on the Plains.
You learn to show sentiments
Without any pains.

Life is beautiful.
Life is sad.
The sentiments are wonderful,
The ones I've had.

The days are lonesome.
The nights are cold.
But I wouldn't trade lives
For riches untold.

I may die a pauper
With nothing to show
For my life on the plains.
But this I'll know.

Money means nothing
When your heart's at rest.
Friendship's the wealth,
Which I have possessed.

So I'll go on living
This life I've begun,
Like the lonesome moon,
I've had my fun.

106

Slinghead Brown

This yarn is about Slinghead Brown. He got that name because he liked to tell stories of his past. I have listened to his stories on the northwest desert country, long after bedtime, and could have listened to more, if I could have stayed awake any longer.

Pop Pate, another one of those old Texas ranchans, told me one time that French Glen, where the hotel was that Pete French built, was the last hole-up of all the old time outlaws and cowboys of the West. He knew many of them. He said on a nice sunny day, there might be 10 or 12 or more old men loafing on the front veranda of the hotel. You could see for two looks across the desert there. If a dust cloud appeared heading toward French Glen; long before it got to the hotel, the veranda population would diminish down to one or two, until it was recognized as friend or foe. I know of some of the escapades of some of their descendants. They all turned into decent, upstanding citizens.

I was lying around Lakeview, Oregon one fall, when my old friend Slinghead Brown spotted me. He wanted to know how I'd like to take him down through Arizona, all expenses paid! I had a fairly new pickup, and was recuperating from my bad horse wreck. I agreed it'd be a whale of an idea.

"Let's go!" I grins.

"Can't 'till the middle of October." was Slinghead's answer.

"How come?"

I pestered him until he explained. His 25 year parole from the "Florence Bar College" wasn't up until October 15. If he was caught with one foot in Arizona before the 15th, they could force him to spend the rest of his days there. He was another of those old time cowboys that got paroled to spend the rest of their days away from Arizona.

An old time cowboy motto went something like this. "Live fast, die young, and make a good looking corpse." My friends Casper, Dean, and Boots, and many more did it that way. If I'd known I'd have lived so long, I'd of taken better care of myself when I was younger.

Slinghead was a cowboy's cowboy. He reminded me of those old "out Our Way" cartoons in the Western Livestock Journal newspaper - of the old cowboy saddling up a bronc, with a hind foot tied up. Under the heading, as I remember, it said something like this: "When I was young, I took the rough edge off for the old cowboys, but now days I have to take the rough edge off for the young cowboys!"

I first knew him in 1948 on the ZX in Paisley, Oregon. He was the wagon boss on the second wagon, a "greasy sack" outfit, sent to gather the high desert. Six of us gathered over 2,000 two-year old replacement heifers on an area covering about 150 sections in about six or seven days.

The first night in camp, we were saddling to make a short circle to see what we could see. I didn't have a string cut out to me yet. Slinghead said, "Catch that sorrel." I pitched my Houlihan on him and started toward my riggin'. No one told me his name was "Jerky." Before I knew what was happening, Jerky whirled and sold out, and I couldn't hang on to my "lass" rope.

The last I saw was him in a dust cloud, vanishing; but there was a man ahorseback building after him. A while later, here comes Slinghead on a lope, bringing my horse back. He had a few scratches. I asked, "How'd he get all those scratches and cuts?" He answered, "Just as I caught up to him, he jumped the fence. I roped him before he got to going. I whirled my horse around, and drug him back over the fence!" I just grinned, and got my bridle on him, before I took Slinghead's rope off, and says, "Thanks!"

The last I knew of him, he was breaking horses for a Gardner, Nevada cow outfit, after he was way past 65 years old!   I heard he got bucked off, and he splattered like a rotten egg.

"I take my hat off to him!"

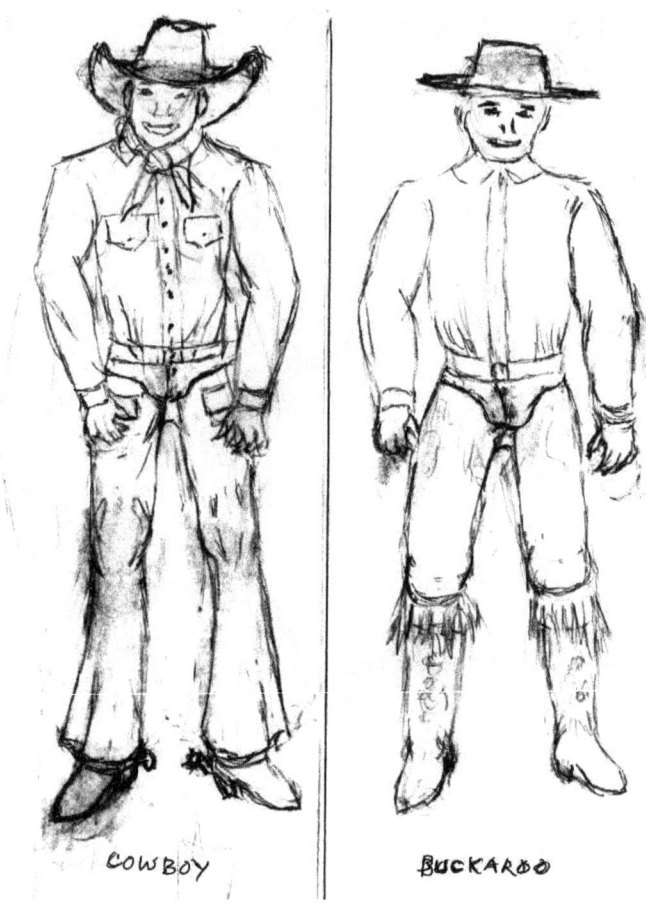

Cowboys and Buckaroos

The ZX ran a cowboy crew from 12 to 30 or more. The wagon pulled out of the winter quarters, heading to the desert sometime around the middle of March, depending on the weather. It took a couple months to get them all scattered around in several pastures, which ran in size from the smallest which was my fenced in wrangle trap of 14 sections. (A section being one square mile, or 640 acres); to the largest which was 50 miles wide and over 100 miles long, with no fences, just natural boundaries. By then, it was time to start moving the cattle to the high country of Sycan Marsh, which was over 100 miles from a city. No trips to town. We spent a couple months branding and shipping out of Sycan, by train on the logging railroad.

Then it was fall; and time to start drifting them down off the mountain toward the Chewaucan Marsh to winter quarters. Paisley, a town of less than 300 people, was about 50 miles from Lakeview. I was with the last trail herd shipped out of Lakeview, Oregon by train, while working there.

I remember an article I read at that time, stated that there were 11,000 single men in Lake County, Oregon. The big majority of these were loggers, but farm hands and hay crews, as well as cowboys, buckaroos, and sheepherders were included.

Most of the wagon crew camped together in places like the "Buckshack", sorting, shipping, and moving cattle all winter. We never fenced, fed, or did anything afoot, except shoe our own horses. But even then, I've shod or helped shoe some old cowboy's horse for him. Like right now. I wish some young puncher would come along and help me with my horses' feet. Shoeing is hard work, and my old 'sacroiliac' ain't what it used to be.

Back in those days, if you couldn't get it done ahorseback, they'd send a "rosinjaw" out to fix the problem. In the Northwest, all ranch hands, other than the cowboys or buckaroos, were called " rosinjaws." They butchered and ate old cow meat. The wagon crew ate prime yearling heifers that were still following their mothers.

I guess I should tell those who don't savvy, the difference between old time cowboys and buckaroos. The ZX was a Cowboy outfit, and the MC was Buckaroo. I worked on both ranches and had good friends in both places.

Cowboy crews used grazer bits on their bridles, double rigged saddles, and short 50 or 60 foot grass or hemp ropes. There were a very few 35 foot grass ropes even on the ZX cowboy outfit, except maybe in the summer during branding. That was before nylon came into production.

There was also a little difference in their hats, chaps, and gear. Cowboys' hats were mostly high crowned with a crease, and a roll up in the front quarter of the brim. Buckaroos' hat crowns were lower, flat or round crowns, with the brims flat or turned slightly down.

Buckaroos used spade bits on their bridles, rode single rig saddles, mostly centerfire saddles, and a rawhide riata. Eighty-five feet was a short rope for them. Some of the buckaroos I knew used up to 125 feet of rope. Why the long ropes?

Cranky horses, slick, muddy, or icy ground, that you couldn't always set a horse up and turn him after a roped cow , which required a lot of rope to play with; so you didn't get your horse jerked down or lose your rope.

They wore "chinks" which hung down just below their knees. Cowboys most all used "batwing" chaps full length, or occasionally a pair of "shotgun" chaps, which were fitted more snug down the legs, without the extra flap of the batwings. A lot of the buckaroos used long tapadero covered stirrups, whereas a lot of the cowboys' stirrups were open, narrow, and even oxbow type. But we all did the same kind of work, and all ahorseback.

I sort of came up with the cowboy way of doing things, but in my travels, I picked up what I figured were good ideas. One was learning to "dally." I'd been home near Pueblo, Colorado to a rodeo. A big bull ran through the fence and was heading for the grandstand, when one of the pickup cowboys roped him. The bull whirled and charged the roper. It took several whirls and kicks to get away from that bull before another pickup man also got a rope on him, to keep him away from the first roper. I'd seen some good dally stackers in similar circumstances get away from such predicaments because they could whirl and coil up their slack, and be able to get away and jerk the belligerent bull down.

I watched and thought. Had that been a dally man, he could have coiled his slack and handled the situation differently, instead of trying to hold his slack from the tied horn loop as high as his arm could reach, to keep his horse from getting over the rope before help got to him. I decided right there, when I got back out in the northwest, I was going to learn how to dally.

I don't know how many hundreds of sage bushes, rocks, and imaginary calves throwed at, jerked my slack, and took my turn on the horn, before I decided I could rope a live animal and dally.

The first time I had to dally, I was after a two year old steer that needed doctoring. When I rode up and snared him, I was thinking I had my grass rope tied hard and fast to the horn, but when I set my horse up to stop him, as we were getting into some rough, rocky country, where I figured I could not get by him to trip and bust him. Lo and behold! My "tied" loop around the horn, came undone, and there he went with my rope!

When I got him hazed back out into open country, I thought I could ride up close, pick up the rope with my toe, and get my hand where I could dally and do my job. Every time I got up close to get my rope, my horse would shy away.

Finally, up the way we were heading, I saw a good round rock, not too big around, sticking up out of the ground a couple feet. I thought if I got up close enough behind the steer, I could set my horse up some, step off and dally around that rock. I was much younger and more active then, than I am now, in my mid- eighties.

So I got up close, set my horse partly up, stepped off him, grabbed the trailing rope, and managed to get my short rope a couple turns around that rock. I got him stopped about the same time my partner had seen my predicament and had come to my rescue and heeled my steer.

We got him down and doctored. I got my head rope off before I got my horse back under control. Luckily, I had used a long McCarty, tucked under my belt loop, and was able to get back on before my partner stacked up on the heel rope to turn the steer loose.

That wasn't the last time I ever used a loop tied hard and fast, but I got a longer rope and really started practicing dallying seriously.

A Gallopin' Goose

One afternoon during harvest at the MC, I got an urgent call to get the road grader and head five or six miles down to Warner Valley. There was a fire in the Barley Field where they had just started combining. The call said ASAP!

Have you ever seen a road grader gallop? Well, I had 'er galloping full tilt! We were only hitting the ground now and then.

By the time I got to the field, one of the combines that had a full bin of thrashed barley, saw the fire and dropped his unloading augur, then poured a furrow of thrashed barley around the two to five acres that was burning. That slowed the fire down from spreading.

There was one of the men there that also knew how to run a grader. He came running, jumped on the grader, as I was plowing a furrow, and said he'd take over. There was an extra pickup there for me to grab it, race back, and get the big 10 wheeler water truck. We got the fire under control about dark.

Another days work!

A Good Cook and a Mule Skinner

I don't remember his name, and I don't know if I ever knew it. We just called him 'Tucson'. If he'd graduated from the Iron Bar College in Arizona, we'd probably have called him "Florence".

Hank McDaniels was the wagon boss and he'd hired this old stove-up cowboy for the wagon cook. He'd been around enough wagons to know what a wagon cook was. He was nothing extra good or bad; but he showed us right off he was a mule skinner!

It took several cowboys to get those mules harnessed and hooked up after they'd rested all winter. This was the first move in the Spring. Tucson was up on the front of the wagon box, standing up checking the lines and the rigging to his satisfaction.

Hank rides up and says, "I think if you ease them off they'll be OK". Tucson nodded OK and for the boys to turn them loose and stay out of the way. He raised all six lines as high as his head and squalled like a panther as he slapped them down. He "eased" them off at a dead run! That Buckshack field was most nearly a section and pretty smooth. About two turns around that field and those mules settled right down. He didn't have any trouble with them the rest of the season.

Chuckwagon Cook

He was always the first one up
And had coffee waiting, but you had to get your own cup.
He could drive six head of cantankerous mules,
And he lived by the chuck wagon rules.

He stayed on his side of the fold-down
Where he'd put meat and 'taters and dough-gods golden brown.
With the round-up tub under the table;
Sometimes we'd help when the weather was a bad fable.

But stove-up as he was,
He was still the best, and the chuckwagon boss.
How we hated to think how he got there;
But we thanked that old outlaw hoss.

He was just a chuckwagon cook
Cause he couldn't ride a horse no more.
A bad wreck out in the malapais
Left him mighty broke up and sore.

But a man has to work to eat.
And the old wagon cook had met his final defeat.
He says, "You just betcha your boots,
I can spoil grub with the best of them, until the old owl hoots."

120

Ranch Cookin'

Ranch cookin' is different from city cooking. They're about as far apart as "McDonald's" is from a fine New York City restaurant featuring "French Gourmet Cuisine."

To start with, it has three meals a day; breakfast, dinner, and supper. That means three "squares;" not coffee at 10 in the morning, cottage cheese and corn chips for lunch, cocktails and a rich meal heavy on the calories, which can only be absorbed by stretching out in front of the TV 'till bedtime.

Ranch meals usually occur from 6:00-6:30 AM for breakfast; 12 noon-12:30 for dinner, and 6:00- 6:30 PM for supper. This varies according to seasonal work, but it's a pretty reliable yardstick.

The second basic is that most of the work is done "from scratch." Cakes are mixed up with flour, sugar, milk salt, and whatever flavoring is desired. Bread is mixed and kneaded on a breadboard, and set to rise in a warm place until ready to bake. Biscuits are cut out and baked. Pies are rolled out and filled with sliced apples, chocolate pudding, or lemon and meringue. All this leads to savory odors that can be carried two miles away, if the wind is right. This only whets the already hearty appetites of the crew, which still has an hour to go before the dinner bell rings!

122

Wagon Cook

I never ever hired out as a wagon cook, but the job was forced on me temporarily several times. I'd worked as a horse wrangler on several outfits. On a big cow outfit, the horse wrangler is also the cook's flunky. If the cook is 'under the weather', he leans heavy on the wrangler, who sometimes might even have to get the next meal ready.

One early winter about the middle of December, I was appointed the wagon cook on a winter gather of the last herd to move out of the mountains. We had line camps to stop at; so we just used the mobile greasy sack wagon to move our food and beds from camp to camp.

We got the herd gathered; a couple thousand or more dry cows, into a smaller holding pasture. We'd leave the next morning.

When we rolled out in the morning, there was two or three feet of snow on the level. The wagon boss says, "Red, I guess you're the wagon driver. You're the only man in the crew besides me that knows how to circle around and get to Currier Camp; and in this storm I'm not sure I'd know the way. So, we'll see you this afternoon in camp. Have some good hot Chuck ready for us."

The ranch had a 1946 Dodge 4X4 Power Wagon, with big heavy tractor chains on it. Also, besides our chuck and beds, I had a couple 55 gallon drums full of gas, along for "extra."

The cattle trail more or less cut straight through to Currier Camp twelve or fifteen miles. The road, however, circled around 30 or 40 miles up through some higher country covered with timber. Things were OK until I came to this 10 to 20 acre open meadow in the timber. The snow was over 3 feet deep, and it was impossible to see where the road was. I stopped and got on top of my Dodge chuckwagon, and studying the country, decided the road went straight across the meadow five or six hundred yards to a tunnel in the timber that had to be the road. I got a bearing on the trees, aiming for the slight gap in the timber. After 10 or 20 feet, I'd have to stop and back up. The snow boiled up over the radiator on the hood clear to the windshield. I'd clean it off, check my direction bearings and hit the snow again. I finally made it across the meadow, and yes, it was the road I could see good enough in the timber to follow it.

It was getting close to sundown when I pulled into Currier, where a crew of hungry, worried cowboys were nervously waiting for me.

They had a good fire going in the cookstove. I dived right in and in no time I had a meal ready; coffee, steak, gravy, doughgods and desert goulash. Part of being or doubling a chuckwagon cook is being able to put up a good hot meal in a very short time. Hungry men will eat most anything if it has a taste and is hot. If it seems tasteless to the cook when he tries it out, and he has to add some Tobasco sauce to it, that says a lot about poor quality cooking.

I have made many a meal on just desert goulash alone. You start out with sliced or diced potatoes and onions frying in a greased skillet. (Bacon grease gives the best taste.) Then add a can of diced Spam and top with a can of green beans (drain off the juice). If you like, add a couple drops of Tobasco sauce (we didn't know what salsa was back in those days in the northwest country). If you have some pre-boiled spuds, you can skin them and dice them for a quicker meal. Sometimes if you have it you can add a can of tomatoes. It makes a good addition.

We never had a salad. I can't recall of ever eating a salad with a chuckwagon meal in all the years I followed one; from the time I was 16 until I was almost 25, and a few times in later years.

It took 55 gallons of gas to get from Sycan Marsh to the Currier camp. Getting to the next camp, Chalk Hills, wasn't as bad as it didn't snow anymore that night and the wind didn't blow so hard. I had a blazed trail to follow back to the low country; then circle around the mountain to get to the Chalk Hills, 50 or 60 road miles. From there to the Red House was a cinch. I willingly let the ranch cook feed us there that night.

Those cowboys had a good hot ranch meal after they got the herd through the fence and into the upper end of the Chewaucan Marsh meadows.

El Bingo, the Wagon Jingler

A good well-run chuckwagon has to have a good horse wrangler. Of course, you also need good cowboys to make an outfit run smooth. If you get a good boss, a good wagon cook, and a good wrangler; you'll get good cowboys and they'll stay there.

El Bingo, the jingler on the ZX for quite a while, was a good one . (Wagon wranglers have lots of handles from Jingler to horse pimp and so on.) El Bingo was always referred to as the jingler.

He had a mind of his own. One time when he decided to go fishing, as he rode by the 'Rosinjaws' farm camp, his horse started to limping. About that time he spotted a John Deere tractor sitting by the corral. "Heck he decided, I'll just corral my horse and continue the trip on John Deer. It cranked right up; so onward he went.

When he got to the river, he scouted it a ways and finally found a spot that looked good to him. He decided "Right here is where I'll fish." Only it looked better to him out in the middle of the river. Since he didn't have any wading boots, he'd just drive old Johnny Poppers out in the middle and fish from the seat. Just as he got out as far as he wanted to go, old Johnny Deere hit a soft spot and got stuck. Well, he'd just go ahead and fish since he was where he wanted to be.

He was doing real good and had quite a string of fish, when he heard a noise and looked toward the bank. Lo and behold, there sat Buster Vaughn, the ranch superintendent, in his pickup! They sat there eyeballing each other for quite awhile. Finally Buster asks, "Are you having any luck Bingo?" "You bet, I'm doing pretty good." Buster sat there studying Bingo some more, and finally came out with, "I'll send someone down with a big tractor and cable to pull you out." Waving, he drove off.

Everybody liked El Bingo. He didn't even get a chewing out for the shenanigan he'd pulled, not to mention getting fired like some of us could have. That night we had fish on the chuckwagon table. After several inquiries, Bingo finally came out with the story of how he caught the varmints. I can still see his face as he told it, with his eyes shining and a big lop-sided grin, as he held up his string of caught fish!

Where a Cowboy Spends His Pastime

Now I know of a place on the desert
Where all of the cowboys go.
Where there's red lights and women,
And whiskey like water, does flow.

You can pick yourself a maiden,
A tall blonde or a beautiful redhead.
Buy her a drink of whiskey,
And then take her to bed.

Well we were sitting in camp one evening,
When Tom says, "Now let's go to town.
For I long to see that brown eyed maiden
That was dressed in the pink silken gown."

So we put on our fancy shirts,
The ones with snaps made of pearls,
Then we started for "Old Hollywood"
For to play with those brown-eyed girls.

The night was one made for romance.
The moon shone yellow and bright.
And we made love to those beautiful maidens
Until the dawn's pale silvery light.

We told how we hated to leave,
Though we thought we'd best be on our way,
Back to the old ZX and work,
But we promised to return next payday!

The Last Lynching

One cool breezy spring morning Florence Rene, the chore man on a large ranch in southeastern Oregon, set out to do his early morning chores. Florence was a hard up, old time cowboy, a good man and all, but being of a superstitious nature he was pretty excited. He left the bunkhouse, slammed the door, and was making his way toward the cookshack to get the milk bucket. He was stopped in his tracks by fright!

For swinging by a hangman's noose, in the misty light of the early morning, was a body, swaying gently from the ridge pole above the corral gate!

Excitedly, Rene retraced his steps to the bunkhouse to awaken Pat Hurd, another superstitious Irishman, to enforce his courage; so as to have the nerve to inspect the dangling body form.

Rene burst into Pat's room so nervous he could hardly tell Pat what he had observed. Finally, by the time Pat had jerked on some clothing, Rene had gotten his tongue untangled enough to tell him of the gruesome sight.

Pat and Rene came out hurriedly, kicking gravel like long-stepping jackasses. Each was trying to hold back enough so that the other might be in the lead and reach the body first. As they reached the swaying figure, they could read a large sign which was attached to it. The sign read:

Emmet Mapes   1896 -1952
(The pot belly from the Pecos)
Hanged by a committee of Vigilantes
For lying and stealing.
For the good of the community.

Florence and Pat were actually shaking in their shoes when they finally discovered the life like figure was really just a dummy, and not a man. At that, the word got out that Florence was so scared that he had to return to the bunkhouse and drink several cups of black coffee before he could summon enough courage to go on about his chores.

We, the cowboys of this outfit had been camped about a mile from where the hanging took place, and about every day for the previous month, while we were working, Emmet Mapes had come over to our camp, and stolen and hidden little articles of ours.

It began all in fun, but after a while it got irksome; so we told Emmet if he didn't stay away that we were going to fix his clock - permanently.

Finally, the cook, horse wrangler, flunky, and I got together and built this life- like dummy, which I must add was a remarkable likeness of Emmet at a distance. We hauled him over to their camp late one evening where we strung him up. It was a good joke, with some after effects, for we almost got run out of the country.

Emmet's only comments were that he was going to get a big gun that would shoot clear across the meadow, and that some day when he spied us four yahoos together, he was going to blow us clear to Kingdom Come!

Spanish Omelet

I was lost, away outside my normal circle. In the distance, down in the valley, I could see a crossroads with what appeared to be a filling station and restaurant. It was a long way back to my bedground, and it felt like I hadn't eaten for a week. Thinks I, I'll just slip down there and tie up my horse ad wolf down a bite.

It was a nice place but looked a bit Swedish or Scandinavian from the type of decoration. Being away from the south land for quite awhile, I was expecting to see a cute little dark haired, brown-eyed gal to ask what I'd care to have. Instead, blond hair and blue eyes (sure nothing wrong there) appeared, and that confirmed my opinion.

After studying the menu and finding nothing that sounded like south of the border, I asked the gal if she thought the cook might whip me up a good hot Spanish omelet. "She'd ask him", was her answer.

Pretty soon she returned holding a tray way out in front with a plateful of fuming food, and set it down in front of me. Out of the corner of my eye, I spotted the cook peeking out at me. The food was hot for Wyoming, but sorta mild for "South of the Border". I dived right in and after a couple mouthfuls, I looked off to the side and noticed the cook still peeking around the corner. The waitress asked if I wanted anything else.

"You wouldn't happen to have some Tobasco Sauce would you?"

"I'll see," was her answer.

I shook a lot of that Tobasco sauce out, holding the bottle up high enough so the peeking cook could see it come out. I kept on shoveling the food in and smiling at Blondie between bites, while keeping an eye on Cookie. I told her how good it was.

I had enough money to pay my bill and leave her a good tip. I asked her to tell Cookie how good the omelet was,

I rode away, facing a cool wind, with my mouth wide open; laughing to myself, thinking how I'd spoiled that cook's expectations.

Goodby

She stood out like a mountain;
Her memory, sharp as a knife.
Her laughter was like a fountain,
And will haunt me the rest of my life.

I stood by, like a boulder;
Something for her to lean on.
She didn't believe when I told her,
I'd miss her when she was gone.

Today, she sent me a letter;
Thanks for a wonderful time.
Goodby to the West where I met her;
Goodby to this poor heart of mine.

SECTION II

- The Middle Years
  1950's-1970's
- Montana, Colorado,
- Education, Marriage, Family

A Hot Spot On A Cold Night

After spending a long season or two in the north land, my pard and I decided to head south and see how normal people survived in the winter. There were several sights we wanted to see along the way, which included Las Vegas. We saw it. Back then, in 1950, if you blinked twice, you were through it.

There was something we'd heard about Silver City, New Mexico that we wanted to check out; so we took a short cut down through Holbrook and St. Johns, Arizona, and on to Silver City. A drastic mistake in those days in the middle of the winter. We about froze to death, but finally made it there, almost starved. The only restaurant we found open was a little Mexican place. All they had ready to eat was chili. Man, that sounded good, so we ordered two big fuming bowls full.

Having been up north for quite a spell, and not eating any hot peppery food, that was a real experience. It wasn't long until we were hot from our throats down to the toes of our boots! We had to eat it as we were starved and low on money, and that was all that was available.

I've eaten hotter food since when I was chili conditioned, but I'll always remember Silver City. At the time, we thought we were going to disintegrate before we could finish and get out. We couldn't quit until our bowls were empty. You see, that Mexican waitress was standing there watching us and laughing to herself, at the tender Gringo cowboys!

140

Hopi

"Hopi." "That sounds like something a gal would want for her hope chest." It would have taken a pretty tough old gal to have wanted him. "Hopi" was an Alice Greenough type, at least!

Not that I ever figured I was much of a bronc rider, but even my type hits a good lick now and then. It's a real thrill when a cranky horse comes along that looks like a bucking horse to the rest of the crew; that is, he's easy to fit a ride on for some fellers. I rode Hopi 66 times, and he bucked 65, mostly just once each riding. All except one day when he bucked two or three times, but he never bucked me off.

I drawed him out of the "greenbroke" string, the stomper had turned in to the cow outfit along in the middle of January. I rode him most every afternoon for over two months, and I was really getting to like him, and got along good with him, right up to when I quit the outfit.

Hopi was captured out of a mustang band on the big desert, when he was a 3 year old. Ordinarily the outfit never started any horses under five years old, but for some reason they kept Hopi up and the bronc rider started working with him. I guess since he was a well built, good looker, they figured if they started him young, he might get over some of his mustang inherited traits.

One morning Hopi was missing from the string of broncs that the man was handling. The next time anyone knew of him, he came in out of the mountains with the extra broncs when he was five years old.

He got caught and started again, and got rode a couple times. Then he came up so lame, they turned him back out. A couple years later, he spent another short siege in the bronc string, before he gave them the slip again.

Finally, the winter he was 10 years old, he got restrained long enough for the bronc rider to get him started and turned in with the cow outfit. That's when I drawed him.

He wasn't a hard bucker and had no wicked kinks in him. He would usually behave until I got all ready to move off the bed ground. Sometimes I'd get two or three hours in on him before he'd decide it was time for his extra-curricular activity.

Usually he'd just buck if I was trying to head some old cow and was trying to coax a little more speed out of him. But not always.

One bright sunny afternoon, when there was an inch or two of slick, slimy thaw on top of the hard frozen earth, was when he figured the time was right.

I rode him in a snaffle, and had a long braided McCarty from a soft nylon rope with loop reins and a long lead shank. Part of the time, I tucked the coil end of the shank under my belt. I almost got weaned of that once, way down in New Mexico by grabbing the tail end as I departed from my trusty steed, straight up into the clouds. I must have sure got a good grip it, as it stopped my upward journey and swung me right out in front to line out that old hide perfect to tromp right straight over me. 'Nough of that, but maybe you savvy now why I didn't always tuck my McCarty end under my belt.

Anyway, I got on Hopi good, clean, and straight up about a hundred feet right out in front of the crew. When I nudged him forward, you'd have thought a tornado had hit him, the way he came to pieces. There was no way he could keep his feet straight under him, the way we came back down in a pile.

We hit the goo, made a big splash, and came right back on four legs, a'buckin. I came up with him in good shape, though I was sort of crooked in my saddle, with one leg way up forward and my foot right under his chin. I couldn't get straightened up, so between jumps I looked to see why I couldn't get my leg back down by his side.

Lo and behold, my McCarty was half-hitched around my left spur about a foot behind his chin!

I remember looking up and seeing the crew all sitting on their horses, grinning and unconcerned, the crew, not the horses. I tried to holler for help, that I was fouled, but I realized they were all on young horses and couldn't do anything, even if they realized I needed help.

I didn't know how I managed it, but on the next jump toward the moon, I managed to reach down with my left hand and get the half-hitch off my spur. Lucky for me I got him doubled out of bucking before his next jump, as I was about give out. And I still had a few hours to put in on him before evening.

Sometimes it is hard to figure out how a horse that has been through as much as Hopi, could still have a good light mouth, but he did.

When I was young, I learned that I could ride and get along with a lot more cranky horses if I could double them than I could by riding and letting them buck whichever way they wanted. I learned if I could stick a cranky horse's nose under my armpit, then I had the battle in my back yard instead of his. I don't know if it was the smell that slowed them down. I just believe a horse can't buck much with his nose yanked back up by your saddle swells.

I guess the reason I sort of liked Hopi was because he never ever got me bucked off. Most of the cranky horses I've ridden have bucked me off about half the time, if they got a good run at me.

There's a great thrill to have a horse that shows good but is easy to ride, but even that has its limitations. Some slow times, when we weren't on the full gallop to keep the work caught up in the winter, the boss would pass out a can of louse powder to each man in the morning. This one morning, one of the few mornings I rode out on Hopi, the boss passed out the louse powder. I thought to myself, "Boy, I sure saddled a good horse for this kind of a day! Oh well, what the Hell!"

The day before, I had come in across the meadow by myself, and had found a cow so lousy she could hardly walk. I was fairly close to the corrals so I managed to ease her up into a big lot. I saw the boss that evening and told him what I'd done, putting the lousy cow in that corral.

We lined out that morning and when the boss stepped off his horse to open the gate into that lot, I couldn't get Hopi to settle down until I got to the end of the line of seven cowboys. I knew what was going to take place soon.

The boss stepped back on his horse, built himself a loop, jumped out a short ways, and hung his loop on that old Sooky's horns.

Would you believe that six cowboys that were all better ropers than I was, rode up to that cow's rear end, pitched a loop, and never even picked up one hind foot?'

"What the Hell!"

I had my loop built and was in line and reached out and snared both hind feet, just as Hopi pulled the plug! I got my turns and reached up and grabbed the off rein just as old Sooky was jerked about six feet off the ground. Well, here we come back by her rear end, me coiling the slack in my rope and Hopi pawing up the earth. As we went by her rear end, I guess she hit the ground so hard she never tried to kick out of the rope.

I took my turns again, and as we hit the end of the rope again, I got Hopi doubled back by her. This time I had to throw the slack over my head to keep from getting tangled up. As we bucked back past her, I got my rope in position and got Hopi doubled again just as we hit the end.

Lucky for me, Hopi quit his pitching and looked down the rope like the good pony he was. We sat there and held her while some unfortunate cowboy had to get off his horse and go powder old Sooky.

I ran into the wagon boss recently, and of course we hashed over lots of cowboys and ponies in our half day's visiting. Finally I got around to: "Whatever became of old Hopi?"

"'Well, he says, "After you left I turned him to a couple different fellows, and he just went from bad to worse. They couldn't get along with him, and I finally sold him that fall."

Saddlebronc - Rye, Co Rodeo 1953
Red Cloud

Bronc Riding

They say he is risking his life.
Boy, he's sure taking a chance.
Look at him on that mean bronc!
Hasn't that fellow got any sense?

He's slipping to one side.
Oh! There goes his hat!
But now he's up straight again!
Gee, I wish I could ride like that.

Look at that bronco go high,
I'll bet he's doing his worse.
If that cowboy can stay two seconds more,
I'll bet' ya he takes the purse.

Oh, that last high dive,
It gave him an awful bust.
There goes the whistle now.
A might too late. He just hit the dust!

But I guess that's the way it is.
The money seems so near.
But he has a streak of bad luck.
All that cowboy wins is the crowd's hearty cheer!

Monotonous

My first day in college
Was like a bronco in a corral.
Wondered what I was getting into,
Returning to the call of the school bell.

I have spent most of my life
In a country that was big and free.
And to be herded into a room
Was awful hard on me.

To set and hold a roundup
Was work I loved so well.
But to set through a lecture
It's hard for me to tell.

When you live in the open
Where the ceiling is the sky'
You concentrate on nothing in particular
But notice everything that chances by.

Due to my former habits,
It was difficult for awhile
To keep my mind on my school work,
While someone passed notes down the aisle.

Someday I may return like a bronco
To the range it loves best.
After I soak up enough book learning'
To pass a veterinarian's test.

Someday I shall return, but now
I must use my time well.
Although I despise being inactive,
My schooling means more than I can tell.

150

Letter to Jarretts

Pueblo, Co.
1953

Dear Jarretts,

Yes, I'm still alive. Please excuse my stationery, but it's all I have with me. I'll elaborate on what I have been doing since I last seen you. Prepare yourself for a shock. At the present I am supposed to be listening to a lecture in English class. Yes, I said English, believe it or not. I am going to college, studying veterinary medicine.

I am still single. Know any good looking gals that's looking for a lover? They don't know what they're missing.

I had become restless with myself. The old creed of "Live and Let Live," had become boring. I had tried to change occupations, but found nothing suitable.

What should I do? I could go to college, but I didn't have a High School diploma. Maybe they would accept me anyhow. As a last resort, I gave it a try.

I found, to my anguish, that the college would accept me if I could pass a series of tests. I would have to start immediately, in order to find out whether I was capable of college work before enrollment time. It gave me no time to inquire what the test would cover, and hence, no time to brush up. I was very lucky, as I passed everything except English in good shape. Even my English score was high enough to be over the margin.

There I was: the conqueror of one problem, only to be faced by one much bigger, one much more difficult to comprehend. I had no money!

I had spent the summer; my whole life as a matter of fact, living today and meeting tomorrow when it happened.

I fudged a little, though. Every time I got the opportunity, I would grab a few winks of sleep. Most every night, I managed to find an excuse to go home early. I say early, but don't know if I mean early or late, because I never would get home before 2:00 A.M.

My days were in a state of turmoil. Drag myself out of bed at a quarter of seven, shower, shave, and eat breakfast; then off to school to try to perform the art of being a wide awake attentive student. I'd literally drag myself through my morning classes, but would be somewhat revived by a light lunch.

After my last class, I would be worn out again, so would rush home and grab a couple hours of sleep, before I had to return to work.

Somehow, I managed to find time to do some studying, which kept me interested enough in school that I finally gave up my job; so as to have more time to give to my books.

I might say that the reason I have to study more to get a little out of a course, is because I have been out of school so long, but I don't think that's correct. I have begun to wonder if I really knew I was lucky in one respect. I still had two weeks before school started, in order to make enough money to pay a sixty dollar debt that was pressing, and to save enough money for my tuition and books. If the education looked rough, that's when I perform the best. Twelve hours a night straight through until in October, brought me up to the position where I could almost see my way out.

True enough, it was rather trying, working all night and going to school all day, but it was an interesting experience.

Red

A Cowboy's education

Getting used to studying
Is something I haven't learned yet;
But if I don't flunk out
I shall learn before I quit.

I am getting sorta lazy
Going to school at eight;
But sometimes doing my schoolwork,
I stay up rather late.

That chemistry is a problem.
It's something new to me.
It requires all my free time,
But I enjoy the laboratory.

Biology is very interesting;
American Democracy is O.K.
Physical Education is required,
But English is the class of the Day!

Some days I long for the deserts,
That I have rode across in the past.
I long for the lonesome solitude
Of the mirages and shadows they cast.

To Mrs. Stinson

My dear Mrs. Stinson,
As you read these lines,
Please overlook the mistakes
And be liberal with the fines.

A five hundred word theme?
My, what a chore!
About our days at school
Or what we're preparing for.

Well now, I've wracked my brain
For an idea for my theme:
And not one little thought
Can I find for my scheme?

I suppose I might write
How I spend my long day,
Or possibly I could tell
Why I'm going to school, do pray.

I might even mention
And I'm sure you'd agree
About the many funny moments
That happen here at dear old P.J.C

Why not tell of the parasites
With their many funny ways?
How they give you a sad story,
Why they're not prepared these days.

I could write about the kids
Those with the peculiar style,
Or perhaps a pretty girl
One with a Pepsodent smile.

155

Talk about my teachers!
Enough to fill a book;
But to keep them contented
This idea I'll overlook.

I have kicked these ideas around
And have perceived a thought at last.
I shall compare the days of school
With some of my wild free past.

Summertime Romance

My first year of college started in the fall of 1953 and ended in May 1954. I found a job for the summer at the Don K Dude Ranch about 20 miles outside of Pueblo, Colorado where I was living and going to school.

There was a small dining room off the kitchen for the hands that worked there. It was on the back side of the lodge.

A few nights after I got there, that spring, after school had finished; I was walking by it on my way to my bunk quarters. Something caught my eye. There was a very pretty, well- built gal in there, working around the table. I stood there admiring her and thinking: "Here I was almost 25 years old and didn't even have a girl-friend. I ought to get acquainted with her."

About three months later that fall, we got married.

Marge's Version

I graduated from the University of Omaha in 1953 with a major in languages. I was offered one job in a large insurance company, which I knew would be strictly a desk job, but I didn't want to stay in Omaha; so I turned it down. I applied to a lot of different places, for almost a year, but the only one needing my qualifications was outside the United States. I didn't want to live in a foreign country.

I decided to take a summer job; so I applied to one I found listed in the Union Pacific train brochure, which my mother still had from a trip we'd made the year before to visit her sister in California.

I received a reply within a week, offering a job in Colorado at this dude ranch. I arrived there May Day, 1954. Two weeks of getting acquainted with the ranch owners and other employees, and I was enjoying it.

I was standing in the newly remodeled guest dining room, looking out through the large windows which showed the driveway to this building which was the main lodge. I saw a sky blue convertible, with the top down, drive up and stop by a nearby fence.

A cowboy dressed man stepped out, wearing a big black hat. That caught my interest as I wasn't used to seeing western hats.

We had our first date two weeks later, going to a movie in town. By the middle of July, we got engaged. From then until the end of August, letters to and from my Mom and me, arranging wedding plans, were almost daily!

Red and I went into town one day, and I found a wedding dress that just suited me, and I bought it. Paid cash, which I'd earned from tips from the guests.

About the first of September, Red and I drove back to Omaha in one day, and had a few days to get everything ready. My mom's house had two bedrooms; one with twin beds where she and I had always slept. The other bedroom just had a single bed so Red stayed in it.

We were married in Plymouth Congregational Church in Omaha on Sunday, September 5, 1954. Mom and I had gone there for years. It wasn't a large church, but it had a wonderful pipe organ; that many of the larger churches didn't have.

There were over two hundred guests, between relatives, all Mom's teacher friends, and all my sorority sisters.

We had a lovely reception in the basement of the church. Several of the guests told Mom it was the prettiest wedding they had ever seen.

The next day, we spent packing up our wedding gifts and loading them in Red's convertible. We headed north and west for our honeymoon.

One of the highlights of our trip was him taking me up to Sycan, where the ZX cowboys were camped for the summer.

My Heart

Oh, I gave my ring
And I gave my heart.
How beautiful she sang
When she said we'd never part.

So snuggle up close.
Put your little hand in mine;
For I love you the most
And I have all the time.

So I love you my dear,
Look up in my eyes
For I'll always want you near
And thrill me with your sighs.

And I'll never let you go,
And I'll never make you cry.
And my love for you, I'll share;
So please, darling, let me try.

That was long, long ago,
And the years have come and gone.
And I still love you so;
And your beauty lingers on.

Oh I gave you my heart,
And I gave you my ring.
You said we'd never part!
To your mem'ry, I'll cling.

Just Riding Along

As I went out riding
One cold winter day,
I saw a slim cowboy
Riding my way.

As he rode near,
I was much surprised.
A most beautiful sight,
There before my eyes.

Long auburn hair
And sweet kissing lips.
A Beautiful body
With a gun on her hips.

"Howdy cowboy,
Was what she had to say.
"It's great to ride
On such a beautiful day."

"What are you doing
Out here on the plains?
I see you're a long way
From your home range.

"Riding the chuck lines."
Was all I could say.
"Looking for work
Out this a' way."

"Do you happen to know
Where I might land a job?

At breaking horses,
I'm not a slob."

She looked at me
With a smile on her face.
She said "Follow me home
To our little place.   **Red Cloud**

Dad needs a man
To break some raw colts;
He's been busted up
From too many jolts.

We've tried one or two
That didn't measure up.
You're welcome to try
Your luck, for a "cup."

"Sounds good to me,
Lead the way straight and true.
Inside their corral
Were some outlaws I knew.

I roped about four,
Tied each to a post.
Let them struggle all night;
Wear them down the most.

Tied up a foot,
Brushed them out good.
Saddled and mounted
Like a cowboy should.

The first ten miles
Were rough and wild;

But another twenty
Brought them home more mild.

We worked them on cows,
I taught them to stand.
I earned a place, a job,
And some good land.

The girl is my boss,
My wife and helpmate.
She doesn't sass me
If to dinner I'm late.

A fine life we share
On a ranch we love;
Good horses and cows;
Thanks to Heaven above.   **Marge**

A Cowboy's Ranch

Montana has always been an exciting and interesting land. I liked reading those old trail driving yarns about going north. The worst problem was, it was hot and sticky in the summers, and freezing cold in the winters. But there were then, and still are, some big outfits up there. The Antlers at Wyola was one I drifted to long years ago.

You have heard me talk about the Montana Greenoughs. Alice and Margie were World Champion Women Bronc Riders. Turk Greenough was Men's Champion Bronc Rider. Bill Greenough never rode professionally in the rodeos, but I've heard that he could outride all the other Greenoughs. The worst problem working for Bill, who was the Antler wagon boss, was he expected a fellow to be able to ride the same horses he could. The old-timers say Bill could ride horses that Turk might find hard to fit a ride on.

I stopped in at the Antlers headquarters early one June afternoon, looking for a job. Bill and his wagon crew were out putting a herd together that they were leaving with the next morning, heading for the

Big Horn Basin. He'd left word he needed another hand if one came along. The ranch boss said he'd haul me out to the wagon.

That sounded good to me. We got there about 11:30 that night. I didn't hardly have time to get my bed warm until the cook was yelling, "Roll out! Roll up! Roll out! Roll Up!

Bill cut me out a horse from the extra remuda, and we started the herd up country. They had a quarter section trap up ahead somewhere, but we didn't make it before dark, so we had to night-herd. I drew one of Bill's personal horses for a night horse, that he said was a good one for that kind of work. He and I would take the graveyard shift. Someone would come to relieve us about daylight. We'd gallop back to camp, change horses, and get a bite to eat before the wagon moved. That sounded OK, but things don't always work out.

About 1:30 A.M., the cattle got restless, and we couldn't hold them. He found me and said since we couldn't hold them, and they were drifting in the right general direction; we should try to hold them together and drift with them.

We had good night horses; so with quite a bit of riding, we were able to keep the small bunches that wanted to split off from getting away. We figured our relief would catch up with us by daylight, but the sun was way up in the sky before the crew caught us. Our relief had ridden out to the bedground and couldn't find us or hear us.

We'd crossed meadow-type land for quite a ways, and it was quite difficult to track us in the dark. They had ridden back to the wagon and roused the rest of the crew. After a quick breakfast and the crew getting mounted, it was light enough to track us from the bedground.

It was about 7:00 o'clock when they caught up with us. Bill and I galloped back to the wagon to find the cook all rolled up, and the coffee pot empty. The horse wrangler was still there, so we got fresh horses and galloped back to the herd.

It was close to noon when one of the hands rode by and told me Bill said for me to ride on ahead to where the cook had stopped, and had some grub ready. About that time, one of those heavy Montana mountain fogs came up out of nowhere and hung on for about an hour. It took everybody to hold the herd together, with lots of hard riding.

About the time the fog started to thin out some, I spotted the wranglers' rope corral with the remuda in it, and saw the wagon a little further on. My horse was about worn out. The wrangler pointed out a big stout bay extra horse I could catch and ride.

By the time I got to the wagon, the fog started to build up again. The cook had a large platter of good looking steak and homemade bread on the back of the fire. There was other things too, but I just got a big steak and two slices of bread to wrap it in. I got back on my horse so I could find the herd before I got lost in the fog.

It finally blowed away, and for awhile the cattle moved along real good. Then the sun came out so hot, the cattle started stopping and lying down. You'd get a little bunch up and moving while a bigger bunch laid down.

Finally about 4:30, we had about 500 head stopped and lying down. One of the boys said it looked like we'd have to night herd again, as it was still 12 or more miles to the drift fence.

I thought about it for awhile. I'd worn four big stout horses to a frazzle with very little rest myself.

I decided I'd try a new trick. I had a full pommel yellow slicker rolled up on the back of my saddle, with the collar rolled to the outside. I'd tied it on with packers' slip knots. All I had to do was pull the right string on first one side then the other. Then I worked the slicker with my right hand behind me until I got a good grip on the collar. All this time I'd been working into the herd. There were cattle all around me when I jerked the slicker around to my right side with my hand about as high as my head. The slicker rolled full out.

With a squall as loud as I could muster, I drove the steel to old bay. He jumped about as high as the sky would let him. He hit the ground bucking, with me yelling and flapping my slicker. I was spurring like the devil to stay on top of old bay.

I put so many cattle to moving that two or three or four of the other boys grabbed their slickers and joined me. Our herd was 1,000 or more 2 year old steers that were going out to grow some more. At that time some of the ranches still held steers to 3 or 4 years old before shipping.

We got to where we could turn them loose just before dark hit us. With a full belly, our old soogans really looked good that night.

Bill sent me out to the Shoulderblade line camp. He said there were enough horses out there I could ride until the wagon came out to work that country. He'd cut me a string when they got there.

I don't remember (or maybe don't want to remember), but some friction came up between Bill and me a few days later when I came into headquarters to see him. We argued for awhile. All the time, each of us was getting more het up. Finally he told me I was fired.

"Go into the office, draw your time, and get the hell off the Antlers!"

Somehow, the way he put it, I became more riled. We were standing close, eye to eye. My words were, " Like hell! If you're firing me, you go get my check and bring it to me."

We stood there toe to toe, seeming like a long time; glaring at one another each daring the other to bat an eye or flick a muscle. Finally Bill says, "To hell with it. Get on back to camp out of my sight."

Several days later, the wagon pulled into the Shoulderblade and set up camp. Someone came and told me we would make a gather that afternoon as soon as the cook fed us. I showed up with my saddle. Bill cut me a big strawberry roan 'Applesauce'. His reputation had preceded him. He was hard to saddle; hard to get on, and pretty apt to pitch if you got on him.

What the hell. Bill was setting me up. I kicked that old pony in the guts and acted like I was going to eat him. Jerked him to a standstill and saddled up without him moving. I was irritated, no doubt, and decided on immediate action. I never even tracked old Applesauce. Something you always do. Right then I just gathered him up and stepped right up in his middle, squalling like a panther. Grabbing both shoulders with my meathooks, I brought the double of my long heavy split reins down across his underside. He left the earth, but he hit the ground running instead of bucking.

I made a short circle around camp and got him pulled up about the time Bill stepped on his horse. We all left in a lope. We rode to the highest end of the highest ridge in the pasture, eight or more miles away. Bill turned facing the crew and told one of the hands to take this fellow down that steep draw and push any cattle we found on out into the flats where we'd hold our roundup. I thought it odd that the rest of the crew sat and studied the lower country as my pard and I started.

Bill knew another of old Applesauce's favorite tricks. He liked to buck and stampede on a steep down- hill. He just bellered like some bucking horses do, and leaped out into space, dropping 20 or more feet that first jump. He did it so hard and fast, he jerked both reins right out of my hand. I was riding a flat Denny Hunt tree Hamley saddle with a 1/2 inch cantle and a low A Fork in front. As we were falling towards the sloping earth ahead of us, I remembered thinking I wasn't bucked off yet. My horse was still under me and between my legs. I went to hooking and clawing and yelling to keep up my nerve.

By the third jump down that grade, I'd gathered up both reins and picked up both stirrups. I was still astride when I got him pulled up about a quarter mile from where we'd started.

That Shoulderblade pasture was about 18 miles long and about 10 miles wide. In the middle of the summer, the grama grass would polish your boots ahorseback on a lot of it. There was over 3,000 steers running in it. We were gathering prime cattle to ship by train to Omaha. There was a section fenced in at my camp which was near the middle of the pasture.

We made three circles a day, saddling in the dark of the morning and unsaddling after dark at night. That sure don't leave much bed time in Montana in the summer. We started working the country at the north low end, trailing the cut to my holding pasture, and kicking the rest of the herd behind us, below the country we'd work the next day.

Finally, we had about 650 fat steers worked out. This one morning, Bill said for me to take his son, 14 or so, and another boy and move the cut on down the country to the Benteen shipping and holding pasture. It was only about ten miles. No problem. We got the steers gathered and out of the holding trap, and up in a big open valley with ridges on both sides. I had scouted and high-pointed every chance I could, and there were no cattle in our way. Suddenly, off to our right, up about to the middle of our trail herd, over the ridge came about 200 head of the cattle we'd culled out over the past days. They were maybe 200 yards away when I saw them. I'd sure as hell get fired if I let that bunch back in the fat herd.

If we could spook our herd into a run, maybe I could turn those other steers away and up country behind us. The boys really pitched in yelling and rope-burning the drags. They broke into a good run . I circled around and hit the loose cattle at the right angle at the point and got them turned, on the run. Two herds running away from each other was a beautiful sight to me right then.

The weather was so hot our fat steers slowed back down to a walk as soon as we quit pushing them hard. It was a relief to get them into the Benteen trap.

There was a couple bands of mustangs of 15 head or so, that ran in that Shoulderblade country. The horse wrangler lost three head of saddle broncs out of his remuda before he got to my camp.

After we shipped the train load of cattle out of Benteen siding (which incidentally was the last train load of cattle shipped from there); Bill told me to get those three saddle horses picked up. That don't sound like much of a job, but three old renegade horses in a country with two bands of mustangs in it, is a different story.

The next morning before the wagon pulled out, Bill pointed out seven horses from the remuda for me. I houlihanned six of them out of the remuda without missing a throw. I couldn't locate the seventh one. Finally Bill wanted to know why I didn't catch the last one.

"I can't locate him."

"He's standing right there."

"Well I'll be damned."

The sun had come up and he'd changed colors. I caught him the first throw. A whale of a record for me. Catching seven head out of a remuda of 50 or 70 horses without missing a single throw.

I tried my string in the next few days. A couple of the grullas were a little hard to fit a ride on. One sorrel was some hard to get on. I rode fence on him. Left camp about sunup. When I got to the perimeter fence, if a staple was out, I got off to fix it. If I saw one out on the next post, I'd mount old sorrel and ride him to the next post.

Along about the middle of the afternoon, I was about give out fighting old sorrel, getting on and off him a couple hundred times. He didn't fight me getting on. I rode to the next place to fix, dismounted; and when I remounted, he didn't flinch again. I rode to camp the winner.

Another horse I drawed was a black, over 17 hands tall, with a lot of Thoroughbred in his background. He could buck a little, but I could ride him most of the time. One day I loped out a narrow ridge, and pulled up at the edge to see if there was a way I could get off to the lower country.

Old Highpockets solved the problem for me. He merely leaped off into space with a drop of probably ten feet or more on a steep down hill grade, and went to pawing his head.

I could see a more level clear spot about 75 or 100 yards down country, in line with the direction we were stampeding.

When we got there, I kicked my feet ahead and hauled back on my hackamore reins for all I was worth. Wouldn't you know it? Instead of snatching his head up, it jerked me right down his neck and over his ears. I kicked my feet free and lit on my feet right in line in front of old Highpockets; but my body was traveling faster than I could get shank's pony to going.

On my belly sliding down hill about 40 MPH, I couldn't out-distance that black tornado. He stepped all over me and in the middle of my back. It felt like at least a dozen hooves before he got on over me. I had a long hair McCarty, but instead of having it tucked under my chaps belt, I had it coiled and tied to my saddle strings.

I watched that saddle jerk and bounce for most of a quarter mile before it hooked a sage brush stout enough to stop it and old Highpockets.

I started down country, gathering up my saddle blankets and dripping blood. I still have a scar on my upper lip, under my nose, that I ripped open. I got old High quieted down and resaddled and headed back to camp. It was only about ten miles. It seemed like old High blowed the plug about every mile going back. I shore was glad to get there.

My good wife was in camp. I guess it took her a half hour to pick all the gravel out and patch me up. Montana was a beautiful country, and the Antlers was the kind of ranch I liked and understood; but when the snowballs started falling in early September, I couldn't get Arizona off my mind. I pulled up stakes and moved again.

I guess Bill and I settled our differences. He said, "Red, if you're ever back up this way again, a job will be waiting for you."

East Or West?

Joe was riding along
On a horse big and wild,
When he was stopped by a sight;
One which kept him beguiled.

He was a dashing cowboy
From his spurs to his hat.
He was at home in the saddle
On a horse he called Pat.

Life was so simple
With no worries to bear;
When he met this beautiful maid
With the soft lovely hair.

They rode off together
'Neath the pale moonlight.
She called him her sweetheart
While he held her tight.

They were always together
And he loved her so;
But finally they parted;
So where did they go?   **Red Cloud**

She went to the East
So crowded and busy,
Pushing and shoving,
It made her quite dizzy.

She thought of the West
And the man she had left there.
So quiet and strong;

His life, she would share.

She sent him a letter;
She took a train west.
Won'dring who'd meet her,
Would she be blessed?

No one at the station!
She rented a room.
Asked about the man;
Her heart full of gloom.

They said he's on Roundup,
Be in any day.
Then a rush and a holler.
They came in with their pay.

She waited upstairs
'Till a knock on her door.
She opened it wide,
What she'd been waiting for.

They were married that night;
With the whole cowboy crew
To give their best wishes
And a tepee for two. **Marge**

178

Giddy-up Horse!

Marge in Montana

One nice day in July, Marge went with me ahorseback. She loved to ride, but was not an advanced rider. Her only way of riding where she grew up was to pay $ 1.00 per hour for a one-hour ride at a livery stable on the north side of Omaha. This meant a minimum of two hours of baby sitting at a local neighbor's home, at fifty cents an hours. Then there was a bus ride, and two changes of street car rides (which took an hour each way, to and from home.)

Anyway, we were enjoying the ride. Warm and sunny weather. It began to cloud up. Soon it turned to dark heavy clouds; then started to rain. We were both wearing chaps. Marge was wearing a new pair I had made for her the Christmas before, which was our first Christmas after our wedding last September.

It wasn't cold, but we both put on light jackets, as the wind started to come up. Within a short time, it changed to sleet; then quickly into hail. Big hail! It was pounding on us and stinging the horses.

They went faster, and soon went to bucking from the pellets of hail stones that were hitting them all over. Suddenly Marge was thrown high in the air! She went up about 10 feet off the ground and fell in a heap. My horse was bucking too, but I quickly stepped off, hanging on to my reins, and ran to Marge. Her horse had galloped off.

She was unconscious. I could see that she had a broken arm. I took her chaps off and wrapped them around her arm, holding it in place up to her shoulder. She finally woke up, and I told her we'd have to walk part way back to the cabin. We walked quite awhile, until I found a place where I could drive or car to. She sat down and waited while I galloped back to camp, turned my horse loose, and drove back to where I'd left her. Put her in the car and drove first out to the highway, then to the small town of Hardin to the doctor's office there. The waiting room was full of women, waiting to see the Doc. None of them would give up their place in line, so we sat there and waited for more than an hour.

Finally got in to see the Doc. He checked her out thoroughly. Then said he couldn't fix it. She had to go to Billings to a specialist. It was broken too bad!

I got her in the car and we drove to Billings. It was a hundred miles. Another couple hours. Finally got there, and they x-rayed and studied everything. Said she'd have to stay there for a week or two. They put her in a sort of sling that held her arm out away from her body. Hopefully, it would let the bones re-align to the proper position. After they got her in bed, I went back to camp to take care of my horses, and the job. I had called the headquarters to tell them of the accident, and that her saddled horse was loose.

They let me bring her home after a few days, with her arm in a wide sling that held it out away from her body. Two weeks went by. Took her back to the hospital. New x-rays showed no improvement. They'd have to operate.

Two weeks more in the hospital, and she was allowed to go home. They told her it was healing fine, but she would never be able to reach behind her head again, but all other movement would be fine. The reason for that was nature heals up broken bones larger than the original.

She had broken the top joint of the arm off the main bone, and split it into three pieces. When it healed it wouldn't have room to rotate normally. She needed to do exercises every day for several months to keep it as normal as possible. She practiced this every day almost until Christmas.

The Colorado Rockies

I like to ride away
On a summer day,
To a place I know;
Where the "Quakies" grow;
It's high up in The Rockies.

I hit the old Don K,
And then I'm on my way.
Go in the mountains high,
'Neath a pale blue sky.
So peaceful there, high up in The Rockies.

On a faithful horse
I climb the scenic course,
As the cool breeze sings
To the clear mountain springs;
In my paradise in The Rockies

Then when the day is done
I say, "Adios," to the setting sun.
A day has been spent
Where my heart is content,
In the Colorado Rockies.

My heart'll always yearn
Until I can return
To my vacation stay
There with the old Don K,
In the beautiful whispering Rockies.

Time to Move

I got on with the Quarter Circle Double X. Spent the fall at their summer camp at Williams, Arizona, and moved to their camp near Ashfork for the winter. Back to Colorado. Worked at the Don K Dude Ranch until July of 1956.

Picked up my younger brother, Tommy, and we went back to the ZX. The wagon crew was full, and up at summer quarters, so I took a haying job. Working rosinjaws were getting $5.00 per day, but the outfit needed a man as stacker up on the loose hay stacks. That job paid $12.00 a day. With a pregnant wife, that sure sounded good to me.

I saw in the "Western Livestock Journal" that fall, with just two "loose hay" stacking crews, the ZX stacked 26,000 tons of hay that summer. When haying was over, the wagon was short a man, so I got back on the winter wagon crew. The wagon worked year around with about six months on the desert and mountains, and the other six months handling cattle on the 35,000 or more acres of meadow country.

They had as many as 19 summer camps, some for just short spells, but two or three had longer terms. The longest was the Dominique camp where they ran 2,000 to 2,500 replacement heifers for six or seven months a year, before returning to winter quarters, where the bulls were turned in with them the next spring. The ZX never bred any heifers, on purpose, before they were 2 years old.

The next spring, I managed to draw the Dominique camp again. It was only 96 miles on the section line, north of the ZX headquarters.

I stayed with that system; six months on the desert and about six months in Chewaucan winter quarters with the wagon crew.

The last time there, the boss came by and wanted us to move up to the mountains where they had set up a trailer camp for all the married men.

We didn't want to do that; and we got a different offer from a friend in Bend, Oregon. My feet got to itching, and I had to move on. Again. My last "big ranch" drifting cowboy days were over!

    I had tried several ways to make a living, from driving a propane truck to fixing up a small place with irrigation water for this friend, and buying a few cows at a time for us. We went into partnership with this friend, and another lawyer friend of his, and bought a small run down ranch outside of Prineville, Oregon. Were there for over six years. Our family grew. With our two older daughters Holly and Tammie, we welcomed a son Kip and a third daughter Wendy.

A Whale Of An Adjustment

In this yarn, I'm not trying to tell you that you should go see a chiropractor; it's just about some of the treatments I've encountered in the past 60 years. Once I had a chiropractor tell me it didn't matter how you got the treatment; if it knocked your spine back in line, it was a good treatment! The first such treatment I can remember happened over 60 years ago.

A horse had bucked me off and stood me on my head real hard. My left arm started bothering me so bad I couldn't sleep on my left side at night. If I rolled over on my left side, it would wake me up by hurting. However, when you're young and feel pretty tough, you learn to ignore a lot of discomfort. This went on for quite a while, until one early summer day.

Leppy Mogan and I were galloping a couple broncs across the smooth barren plains east of the mountains in Colorado, without a tree or protection of any kind in sight, when a real wild squall blew up. It started hailing, mostly marble size, but some bigger. A large hailstone would hit our horses on the rump; they'd throw their heads up and quit the earth; but at the same time, more hailstones would pound their heads and ears. Down would come their heads between their front legs until another large one would pellet their rear ends again. I don't remember how long this went on, but it seems like a long time when you're taking a stone beating while you're trying to ride a stampeding horse. I had my reins in my left hand and my right hand probably in the nubbin when my horse lunged and slipped. It threw his head out so extra hard and fast, it like to have jerked me out of my saddle right over his head. In all of that melee, I heard and felt something pop in my neck and shoulders. By the time the storm had passed, my left arm had quit hurting. I was able to sleep on my left side that night. Later, when I got acquainted with a chiropractor, I decided that that had been my first treatment.

Sometime after, I had another horse wreck and sort of hurt my back. I went to a medical doctor and he stuck me in a hospital for two weeks with 20 pounds (it felt like 100) of traction on my legs. He finally said he'd done all he could do; so I hobbled out down the street, stopping under a sign that said 'Chiropractor.' I'd heard of them. What the heck! I'd see if he could help me. After he worked on me for one-half hour or so, I walked out of his place like nothing was wrong with me.

For years, every so often after I'd had several horse wrecks, I'd go visit the local joint popper and get put back together. Years later after I'd quit the cow outfits and had a partnership ranch with some lawyers, I had a wreck. I slipped while getting on or off a tractor, fell, and come up with an awful back pain. I went to the local popper several times (and he was a good one), but he couldn't get rid of my hurt.

It was in the middle of the summer. We had hay cut with a lot of buckloads in the field ready to be stacked. It was on a Sunday afternoon. From the front porch you could see the hay meadows. A bunch of cattle had found an open gate and were messing around where they shouldn't be. I got my two cowboys (my daughters 10 and 12 years old), and we galloped down there to move the cattle out of the meadow. As we got close to the cattle, a big old red Durham bull came up to one of those big

haystacks, and went to butting and hooking it, probably to get the flies off his head and horns.
I was peeved to say the least. I spurred my horse up and whopped the tar out of his rear end with my romal. Instead of him going around the pile of hay, he ran right through the middle, tearing it up, with me right after him pounding on his rear. The bull made it through the hay, but Mickey, my horse, fouled up, turned a flip, and came right down on top of me. I felt I was squashed by the time he got up and off me. I knew I was killed, but I could breathe without hurting, which was something I hadn't been able to do for so long I couldn't remember when. I could move. I dug myself out of the hay and got up without a hurt in my body, except for a few bruised spots. I'd just got another free treatment.

Paulina is a little bitty cowtown way out in the middle of a big wild buckaroo ranch country; like down south where all the ranch kids are swinging a 'lass rope before they can even ride by themselves. The only difference is those northland ranch kids are all packing a buck rein, and are scratching an imaginary bronc from ears to tail. Paulina has their main yearly rodeo celebration over the Labor Day weekend. They had six bucking chutes at the upper end of the arena. To start the shindig, they load all six chutes filled with big stout range cows. A two-man team saddles and halters each cow, and one man gets in the saddle and his partner tries to help line her out. At the blow of the whistle all six chute gates are jerked open simultaneously! There's a starting line in front of the chutes. There's a finish line of lime about 2/3 of the way across the arena. The first team to cross the finish line, jerk off the saddle and halter from the cow and pack them back toward the bucking chutes and across the starter line, is the winner.

Bob Hart and I had won a time or two in the past, but he wasn't there this year. All the leader had to do was get that cow after him, then outrun her across the finish line, and help get the rigging back across the start line. Joe Arnold was going to be my leader; but he couldn't make it.

A good athletic middle-sized cowboy I knew, but had never seen perform, said he'd sure like to lead for me. "Fine, I says, "I'll hold the cow and keep her from hooking you. All you have to do is run like a scared jackrabbit!" He ran scared all right, with old Sooky blowing snot almost in his hip pocket. We were ahead of everybody, and old Sook was in a high run until my leader got boogered, stopped, jerked his hat off and went to batting her. What do you suppose she did? She quit running and went to bucking like a saddle bronc that would have made Casey work to stay in the middle of her. Well, she bedded me down and whirled, hooking, and jumped right in the middle of me.

Oh, I forgot to mention, prior to the rodeo, I'd had a sciatic nerve in my left leg hurting so bad sometimes I could hardly move it. I'd been too busy on the ranch to take time off to doctor it. Well, Old Sooky really gave me a tromping. I was laying there looking for the hide I was sure I'd lost. I finally decided to get up so the crowd would know I was OK. Before I realized what I was doing, I'd rolled over and got up on my left leg. No hurt! It was all gone. I almost felt like telling my leader what a good thing he'd done instead of being mad because he'd lost us the money! Well, if you ever need a good adjustment, come on out to the ranch and follow me around for a few days.

Var la Baine (Forever)

Sometime, when you're
Lonesome and blue.
Look out on the mountain
For I'll be waiting for you.

We'll walk 'neath the moonlight
With your hand in mine.
We'll laugh at our troubles
With our love divine.

And then when you're happy
And your spirits are gay,
You'll know I love you
Though I'm many miles away.

Snuggle closely to me, my darling.
And call me your dear,
For I shall always love you,
And in my dreams, you shall always be near.

I loved you unashamed
With a love simple, but true,
I loved you like an angel
That was sent from the 'Blue'.

All my life you shall inhabit the space
There in my heart;
So again I'll call you My darling,
Before we drift apart.

If ever you need a shoulder,
A crutch to lean on;
If ever you need a friend
When all else is gone.

Then whisper to me, My darling,
A message in the wind;
And I shall appear like magic,
Your love to comprehend.

But now the time has arrived,
When I must say "Adios" again.
So I'll say, "Darling, I love you;
With my "Var la Baine."

Bedroll Cowboy

In the spring, usually around the end of March, the ZX wagon pulled out to the desert with the first herd of 10 to 12 thousand heavy cows. There would usually be around 35 bedroll cowboys with that first herd. Several cowboys were left with each bunch of that first herd to get them spread out on that high desert. Later in the spring, when all the cows were turned out, there would only be 8 to 12 cowboys left with the wagon. In the years I was around there, I had a broken back, and one broken leg, both horse wrecks. The last hitch there I stayed 3 years. A long hitch for a bedroll cowboy.

In between jobs there, I was a bedroll cowboy in Oregon, Idaho, Montana, Wyoming, Colorado, New Mexico, Arizona, and California. These were the ranches I visited in my sojourns.

After quitting the drifting cowboy life, I went into ranching on my own. We bought a small mountain ranch in Colorado. I'd had a lot of experience in my past with big hitches of horses and mules. I'd fallen in love with stagecoaches way back in the 40's, while pulling a stagecoach hold-up in California during a rodeo parade. My pard and I got throwed in jail for that.

Harness horses were almost extinct in the West in the 60s due to all the new 4 x 4 equipment coming out. We liked horses; and had a small band of Registered Morgans; so I started to breaking our horses to drive, in Colorado, for stagecoach horses. My wife bought an old mudwagon which we up - dated for use with our 6-up.

In 1976 for the Bi-centennial, we bought a newly rebuilt Abbott & Downing 12 passenger stagecoach.

By making arrangements a year ahead, with 21 head of horses and our new coach, we traced the old Central Overland Trail from St. Joseph, Missouri to Sacramento, California in 100 days. We had two 6-up hitches and five out-rider horses, plus four others we picked up along the way. In Sacramento, we were given the Key to Sacramento. (It was actually the original key to the jail in the basement of the Wells Fargo office in Old Sacramento.)

In December, 1976, we were invited to participate in President Carter's Inaugural Parade on January 20, 1977 to represent the 17 western states. I felt I was qualified to represent them, since I had worked in most of those states as a bedroll cowboy. I still have my Hamley saddle, a Garcia bridle and my cowboy bedroll. Gave my last pair of Blucher boots to my son a while back.

My wife and I still take the old bedroll with us if we're going where we can enjoy it out in the open country, like we did on our honeymoon in 1954, where we spent several nights with the ZX wagon crew.

And as a footnote to this story, here is an example of "Cowboy courtesy, or manners, or way of thinking, or whatever you want to call it.

We stopped in Paisley, Oregon, and Red went into the post office to find out where the ZX wagon crew was located. They were up at Sycan Marsh, the main summer camp; so we headed there. They were branding calves, so we parked our car out of the way. Red gave me some advice as to camp rules and what "not to do, such as; "if you are ahorseback, do not ride crossing in front of someone else!"

We watched until they were through, and supper was ready. When they were all there, Red introduced me as his wife, saying we had just gotten married a few days before. Then he turned around to me and said, "What was your name?!

The crew was all astonished, to say the least! Then they realized Red was laughing his head off, and it was his idea of a big joke. He finally said, "This is Margie." They all removed their hats, came up to meet me, and congratulate Red.

We all sat down on the ground to have a delicious camp supper. Afterward, they came up and presented us with a wedding present. Seems like one of them had just gotten a brand new tepee that he had ordered some time before, never been opened. They all agreed that each would pay him a share of the total; so he could order another one, and they gave it to us.

Talk about "Cowboy Etiquette!

The next morning, early, as of course, it was a regular work day for the crew, every man in that whole crew had clean washed face and combed hair, and a clean shirt on if they had one. Marge was very impressed, and has told that story many times through the years. She still loves -

"The Cowboy Way!"

Sycan Camp
ZX Ranch

Fall Branding 1954
David Taylor
Wagon Boss

A Cowboy's Romance

Tonight out in a canyon
There's a cool steam running by;
And high on a mountain'
There's a lonesome coyote's cry.

Out over the prairie
'Neath the stars sparkling bright;
There moves a sadness,
You know it just ain't right.

The wind in the trees is whispering
Of a tragic romance.
The tall pines are swaying
For it's their mournful dance.

And there drifts a cowboy
With his head bowed low;
Longing for a pardner
That he misses so.

Once we were so happy
In a world all our own.
We were a happy twosome;
But now I'm all alone.

Once you said you loved me
It made my life so gay.
But now when I need you.
You look the other way.

Somewhere they'll meet again.
Will things be the same?
Will they go their separate paths?

Each one, the other, blame.

 Or, if their love be true,
And troubles be forgot.
A wonderful life for two
As they share Dame Fortune's lot.

My Darling

You make me feel so happy
I could win at any game.
But I remember of our parting,
And I wonder who was to blame.

Sometimes when you're with me
And standing by my side.
I wonder why I left you,
Oh, such foolish pride.

I've lived that parting over
A Million times or more,
And the scar upon my heart, dear
Says I shall never love no more.

For I have made my burden;
My troubles are my own.
For I shall go through life, Dear;
A weary man alone.

Just rambling 'round the country
Is all I ever do.
Searching for something
To take the place of you.

But I know my Darling
As I ramble on my way;
For what I did to you, dear,
All my life I'll pay.

We had such fun together.
You were my shining star.
Though long we have been parted;
I wonder how you are.

Tonight I'm all alone
A-thinking of the Past.
Wondering if you miss me.
Too beautiful to last.

At night time in my soogins,
Out in some lonely place.
I dream we are together,
I can see your smiling face.

You tell me that you love me
And that you'll always care.
For you know I'd rather have you
Than to be a millionaire.

Often you tease me, dear;
Though I think I understand.
For you then draw me so near
And tell me I'm your man.

As I gaze on the Past, My Darling
I think of the sweet things you said,
When you held me to your breast, my Darling;
And soothed my poor aching head.

 Please don't ever leave me darling
It would break my poor trusting heart.
I could never, never go on alone
If we should ever drift apart.

Those tender words haunt me now Darling,
For I know that you were sincere.
Why did I ever make you hate me?
Why didn't I always keep you near?

If you feel the same as I, Darling
And want my love once more;

201

Then answer my letter, Darling
And you'll have what you're yearning for.

Let me be the one to walk with you,
When you want someone to talk to.
The one who means the most,
To sit and share with you.

When you want some loving,
I'll know just what to do.
The pleasures and the warmth
Will be the World for two.

The Hotel Chewaucan was the "Cheyenne Social Club of Paisley, Oregon."

At The Local Waterhole

The Chewaucan Hotel, restaurant and bar was the "Cheyenne Social Club" up in Paisley, Oregon back in those days. The lobby was probably 30 feet square with a big flat-topped and bottomed, straight-sided, egg-shaped stove in the middle of one corner. Two men couldn't carry enough wood at one time, to overfill that stove if it was empty. That's where we were waiting one cold March morning, for one of the cowboys that lived in town to come journey up north with us.

Of course we all had our heaviest coats, chaps, earmuffs, and gloves on. We'd just come in out of the cold and had gotten that old stove to dancing a jig; huffin' and puffin;' but we hadn't gotten warm enough to unbutton yet; when a stranger came down the stairs from the bedrooms up above.

I was standing looking over the stove toward the stairs, and was interested when I saw first some feet, then legs, overcoat covered, coming down the stairs. The expression on his face was comical; white cold and eyes big as saucers!

When he saw us, I guess he made enough noise for the crew to hear and turn toward him. Looking over at us heavy-clothed fellows, he says, "Boy, I thought my room was cold, but you guys must have had one on the north side! We all had a good laugh as we made room for the traveling salesman by the stove, and explained why we were dressed like Eskimos.

It could be the other way too. The hotel, that is. In the summer you could fight the heat and mosquitos 'till way after dark or midnight, but it was a grand old water hole.

One cold fall night or maybe it was winter, as the wagon usually didn't pull in for winter until just before Thanksgiving; anyhow, when I hobbled in that evening, there sat Ray Winters. Back in those days, it was sort of a custom if you were sitting in a saloon and saw a cowboy coming in that you knew, you'd usually have a drink waiting for him when he got there, if you had any money a'tall."

We visited quite a while. Ray'd been out in Nevada at the Spanish Ranch or I L, I forget which. Finally, I got around to asking him why he'd quit last Spring instead of staying on and going to the desert with the crew. He hem-hawed around for a while before he came out with this yarn.

"Well, you remember that last string of broncos I started?

"Yeah."

"That little bald faced stocking-legged sorrel was getting too hard to ride; so I just decided it was time to turn the string over to the wagon crew."

I'm going to stop right here and tell you a little about Ray. He was an inch or more shorter than I was and about 20 pounds lighter. He rode a common old Standard saddle tree and used 26 inch tapaderas. One day, he rode one of his colts, a 6 or 7 year old, up to where I was waiting for some of the crew.

"How's the pony coming along," says I.

Ray just steps off, hands me the reins, and says, "Try him."

I stepped on and loped him out a ways and back. The horse was fine; but his stirrups were so long I had to stick my tongue out, with my toes almost turned straight down to reach them.

I'd seen horses blow up with Ray. He just sat up there unconcerned. If a horse was heading toward a bad place, he'd reach out with his long taps up beside his horse's head and sort of haze him in another direction.

To get back to the story - I sat there and looked at Ray; and came out saying, "With friends like you, I sure don't need any enemies. You turned that horse in because he was getting hard for you to ride, and you can ride circles around me any day of the week, and I drawed him!"

I never was much for asking for any certain bronc out of the new bronc string. I usually let everybody else have their pick, and I took whatever the wagon boss gave me. Guess that's how I wound up with "Rock."

This day, a couple of the crew rode to the Red House corral, picked up the broncos and made it back to the Grain Camp, where we had our winter camp. By noon, the weather had warmed up and there was a couple inches of gooey mud on top of what was still frozen down below. We had a big lot, probably 10 acres, with our rope catching corral located in the opening in front of an open machine shed where we could get out of the mud or cold or wind to saddle and unsaddle.

At the noon table, Grover came out with, "I guess we'll try those colts out this afternoon." He looked at me and grins. "Everything's picked but that sorrel, "Rock" horse. Guess you can have him." I got him caught. I never had seen Ray ride him, but I suspicioned that day that Grover knew what to expect. He was gentle and easy to saddle; no hump, and tracked without any fuss.

There was sort of a frozen dry place in the shade on the north side; so as not to get on with slick, muddy boots. I got Rock out there, gathered him in, and eased right on to him. That is, I almost got clear on him before he fell to pieces.

He throwed his head toward me, and laid out flat with his feet stabbing the other way. The next instant, his head was where his feet had been, and his feet were pointing back toward the barn. I think that by the third jump, I was sitting flat on my rump in the mud, watching the damned thing. I'd only seen bucking like that once, and that was a bull!

He probably bucked close to 150 yards before he hit a slick spot, and was unable to keep his feet going down to make contact with the ground. He went skiing across the rest of the lot up into the pole fence corner.

I can still hear Bill Davis, a friend of mine on a gentler horse who was going to ride with me, saying, "I have finally seen a horse really buck!"

Wouldn't you know some damn fool cowboy rode out, caught him, and brought him back to me!"

This time, I got out more in the opening and pulled his nose around to my saddle horn away from me. While he was flabbergasted, fighting that position, I stepped back on him. I kept his head doubled around as far as I could. He blowed the pin again, but I had him scotched so bad, before either of us knew it, he'd bucked into the rope corral right into the cavvy. I gave him his head, and we made it out with the help of a couple footback cowboys into the opening.

He wanted to run then. I got him headed over the board bridge across the canal, and out into the open desert. We galloped quite a ways before I got him circled and headed back toward camp. He had no bridle-wise savvy at all. Ray turned his green broncs with his taps, as I stated before. That way he didn't harden up their mouths. When he got them broke to ride gentle, then he started to bridle-wise them. He just didn't keep "Rock" long enough to put any kind of a handle on him.

We had a big set of pole corrals on out beyond our rope corral. When I got back toward camp, I took Mr. Rock out there. I got a couple "lass ropes" and taught him to ground drive. I ground drove him several times before I went to riding him again. I even broke him to the gyp line, and gypped him hard before each ride if I had time.

Spring came around, and I was sent back out to the Dominique Camp again. It's a big country, and I was by myself as far as riding was concerned. When I took Rock out on one of those long desert rides, I tried to get the kinks out of him before I left, but it doesn't always come out the way you plan.

One day, 7 or 8 miles from camp, I got off to go through a gate. When I stepped back on him, he throwed that buck at me just like he had that first time I got on him. I was staying astraddle of him, but he was bucking with his head one way and feet the other; then reversing everything the next jump. About the third or fourth jump, he hooked a sagebrush with his front feet as he was crossing over. He four-footed himself as neat as if he'd stepped into a loop. He went head over heels. I managed to get away from him, and had a death grip on one long snaffle bit rein.

Here I was, suddenly lying stretched out lengthwise, parallel with his body, head to head, me on my stomach and Rock straight on his back with all four feet pointing straight up in the air.

I knew he'd fall one way or the other, and I also knew I didn't want his feet coming down on top of me in case he turned toward me. Immediately I flipped and rolled away as hard as I could. He flipped the other way, landed on his feet bucking blind; and sure jerked loose from most of the hide in my hand.

There was a heavy World War II, 4 barb wire entanglement fence off about 100 feet to the side. He hit it full bore, and went right on through, wires just singing and popping. He went a short ways, and stopped broadside to me. There was a whale of a stream of blood coming out of a front leg. My immediate thought was he'd bleed to death before I could even get to him. I gathered myself up off the ground, and looked toward him again as I was hurrying to get there. The bleeding stopped as quick as it had started.

I got through the fence and walked right up to him. I looked him over, and he looked fine to me; so I gathered him up and stepped back on. We went ahead and made a 25 or 30 mile circle that day.

I don't remember how many times he unloaded me, but I know it was more than two. He was one of those few horses that never bucked more than once per saddling. He never bucked twice with me the same day.

I do remember the last time he tried me. I think he gave me everything in the book, but when he quit that day, I was still astraddle.

I saddled him down by the pump house, just outside my pole corral and stepped on. It was just like the first time I tried him that Spring, except now I knew what to expect. I rode with a long set of heavy leather split reins. Every jump he made, I brought the tail end of them with bull whip force down on the under side of his belly. Every jump as he crossed over from side to side, I had to change hands on the reins and whip with the other hand. I missed whipping one jump as I was so far away from the seat of my saddle which was off to the side. If he had gone two jumps in the same direction, I'd have landed on the ground. I reached way out with my left hand and snatched ahold of the horn as he was changing direction of his roll, and jerked him and me right back together.

If you've ever been at the Dominique Camp, you know the pump house is 75 yards or more from the cabin. There used to be an old fallen building off to the side fairly close by the cabin. Rock started at the corral, heading west; made the circle to the north, then east a ways, then south over to the junipers where he quit.

He'd gotten rid of all my saddle blankets, my 'lass' rope, everything out of my shirt and Levi pockets. Everything but me and my saddle were still on when he quit.

I gathered up my blankets, found my pocket knife, my "Bull Durham" and what else I don't remember. I unsaddled, rubbed the sweat marks away, re-saddled, and talked to him. After petting him on the neck, I stepped back on, and went ahead and made my circle for the day.

"Thanks, Ray, with friends like you, I got all the excitement I can stand."

The Privy

The wind got some fierce the other day.
It damn near blowed our toilet away!
Them cowboys should get a medal,
They're so brave and bold.
It takes lots of nerve to hang
Them old balls out in the cold!

Not Quite Broke

"Open the Gate!"

Away across the prairie we went about ten miles or more. I suddenly had to "go" or wet my pants. I got my horse's head doubled up, and stepped off him. I was able to hang on to my caballo.

To get back on became a problem, with him pawing and kicking at me. I'd pulled my right rein across the saddle in getting off. Luckily I had long split reins and was finally able to get his mouth pulled practically up in the saddle, and get a wrap around the horn. With his head pulled around like that, he wasn't able to see me with his kicking and his striking.

I was able to get a good grip of the horn with my right hand, and in between him striking at me with his front feet, and kicking jumps from behind, I was able to vault back in the saddle. I was younger and more agile then. With his scotched nose almost in my lap, I was able to get square back in place to have a good show at him when I turned his head loose. After a couple jumps skyward, I got him back in a lope and made it back to camp, with a half broke horse!

Red's Log - 1957

Jan. 14, 1957.
    Grover and Herb went to Likely, California to look at some horses. I took five men with me, sending four of them to ride the East Jones and Pump House for cows with small calves.

    Tom Anderson went to the House pens with me to pick up a cow and calf which were left, when the cattle were moved after the Red House washed out. She was one mad cow and on the hook. They ran back on us, then to the gate going into the East Jones. I let the calf jump through my loop several times before I could jerk my slack fast enough to keep him. Tom, though riding a bronco was able to drive the cow behind as I led the calf. Things were going fine until the calf fell down and spooked the cow back. I got the calf through the gate and tied up; then went back to help Tom. We couldn't turn the cow; so I roped her, (almost lost my rope). She was quite a load for my horse to drag by himself, so Tom helped. Tom's bronc pulled just like an old timer. It was only about a quarter mile to the gate, and we had to drag her all the way, but things turned out OK.

    Fixed the water trough at the Grain Camp this afternoon, so the horses wouldn't tear it up.

Jan. 15.
    I had the crew again today. Nothing exciting. Happened we got in early. I went to Silver Lake with Grover this afternoon. Looked at the heifers in the Ben Field. The weather looks like a blizzard is coming up now.

Jan. 16.
Rode Jimmykane to the Lower Marsh; worked cattle until noon. Like to froze to death. Ate dinner about 2:00 O'clock.

Jan. 17.
Bunched the North Clover. Roped a leppy calf after several throws with almost frozen fingers. Gathered East Jones and moved them to White House. Late dinner.

Jan. 18.
Bunched North Clover. Went to White House, in pickup with Grover and helped de-louse some bulls that the boys roped outside. Sawed ingrown horns off two or three head.

Got a new horse this afternoon, better than 17 hands tall. A sorrel. Think I'll call him California. Went to rope a beef, but he ran on past, and I got no throw to it. Tom caught the beef.

Jan. 19.
I took stock truck and went to Carlon's at Summer Lake for a load of ZX cattle. Several were very ringy, and I had difficulty in sorting them out in the Red House corrals, (on foot.)

Jan. 20.
No work. Got up late. Made two picture frames for Marge's paintings.

Jan. 21.
Went to Bonanza with Grover to brand some bulls the ZX bought. We branded 59. Stayed all night in Klamath Falls, on the company.

Jan. 22.
Came home over slick highways.

Jan. 23.
I took two men out, and rode to check on some cattle Herb and Drew worked out the two previous

days. Fixed a leak in the water line to the horse trough this afternoon.

Jan. 24.

It was 24 below zero at the cow camp this morning; and three boys and myself were about three miles away when the sun came up. It only shone briefly and then clouded up and really got cold! All four of us froze our noses by the time we reached the Coglon. We then rode through the cattle we worked yesterday, and picked up four calves that had gotten out on us then. We had planned on roping them and leading them back into the weaner lot, but by the time we worked them through the cattle we worked yesterday, with quite a bit of running up to lots, we were so cold, none of us could have roped if we still wanted to. With some difficulty, we worked them with some cows into another field and came around up to the corrals from the opposite direction. We then put our horses in the barn and sat in Grover's house and shot the bull and drank coffee until noon. Ate dinner at the Coglon, and galloped back to the Cow Camp after noon. The thermometer had raised about 40 degrees by then, but still freezing.

Moved the North Clover cattle into the Dobkin's on cake. Left gates open so they could go back to water. Bunched the Higley's and the East Jones on the water grounds at the new troughs in the Red House field.

Vaccinated some more sick horses this afternoon. (Penicillin for distemper.)

<u>Jan. 25.</u>

I had four men. We bunched the cattle in the Dobkin's on cake. Bunched the Red House on the new water. Again moved the South Clover into the 900 acre field. Left the gates open so they could go back to the new Four Corners pump, and then picked a beef out of the Grain Camp field and took it to the corral and butchered it this afternoon.

Jan. 26.

We noticed a large fire in Paisley this morning as we were catching horses. Herb and I kidded about whose house it was, his or mine, but neither of us were very worried. Just as we were riding away from camp, Bradbury drove in and told us it was actually Herb's house. We stood and watched it burn from ten miles away.

The volunteer firemen had gotten most of Herb's furniture in time; so Don Smith and I came back to town and helped Herb to haul it up to Headquarters and store it.

The water was frozen in my house so I came home and worked on it the rest of the day, to no avail.

Jan. 27.

I got up the usual time, and when the bosses came by to pick me up, they told me I didn't have to go to work. So I went back to bed. Water pipes were still frozen.

Jan. 28.

We gathered something over 1,300 head of cows, each with big calves, and took them to the corrals at the Coglon to wean the calves. Wilson, Cross, and I were horseback putting them through or into the chute. I rode Likely. He is quite a horse in the chutes. He towers over the cattle and isn't the least afraid of those horned cows. It took us less than five hours to run the total of some 270 head through. Some cows got into the calves. We worked the most of them out. It was quite a western event.

Two horses fell on the slick frozen ground. Tom Anderson's horse fell early in the morning, and chipped his two front teeth. Cliff Cross's and Dick Reed's horses fell in the corrals. Wilson was after a cow which kept breaking back. Charley threw at her, and a yearling stuck its head up at the wrong time, and hooked a horn in the loop. Charley flipped it to come off, but the yearling jerked his head and the rope came off the cow and settled right around the yearling's neck. I heeled the yearling and Likely quit the flats on me. I got my turns, two of them, but we went right on past the end of the rope, and I lost it (temporarily). Grover then heeled it. I got my rope back and caught the cow. Reed rode up in the way and almost got hooked as I was leading her out of the corral. My saddle was so loose by the time I got through the gate that I had to stop, and the boys had a hell of a time heeling her. Got back to the Cow Camp about sundown.

Jan. 30.

It was only 22 degrees below zero this morning. I drawed a new horse today as Jimmykane has been favoring a foreleg on long rides. I had to hobble Chief, the new horse, to saddle him. He started out alright, but about a half mile away, he broke in two, and almost bucked me off. I had left my spurs off because of being so damn cold, and I almost paid for not having them. I really needed them to hang on with. I had Cliff, Tom, and Don with me. We moved the cows away from the calves we had weaned; away from the Coglon corrals.

Three cows had gotten in with the calves, and one calf escaped while we were getting the cows out. Cliff finally got a rope on him and led him back. We didn't work in the afternoon.

Jan. 31.

I took four boys, Cliff, Tom, Don and Spence, and went to the North Swamp, where we met Grover. We gathered 400 some odd southern heifers and took them to the Harris field with no little amount of excitement. The heifers wouldn't go into the trap at China Town. Some of them kept breaking back and running like jackrabbits,

Finally, one of them, which I was after, was completely determined not to be driven back to the roundup. My horse did all any horse in the outfit could do in turning her. Finally he even got to crowding her with his chest in behind her foreleg; crowding her around in the right direction; but still, she would break back; so I roped her just as Grover rode up on a bronc. He took my rope while I tightened my saddle. Then I took my rope and started back to the roundup. Likely, my horse, blowed up, and I had to quit my rope and use both hands to control him. After making a circle of about half a mile in diameter, I got back to the little cow and managed to pick up my rope. I lost it again under the same circumstances. Grover roped the cow which had become on the prod by then. His horse blowed up and went to bucking. We lost his rope when I tried to take it from him. So, there we were with two ropes on the ground on a cow which was on the prod. I finally rode up and got off and picked up a rope. Likely is about 17 hands tall. While I was off on the ground, the little cow charged, and there I stood with one foot in the stirrup, kicking her in the snoot to keep her from hooking my horse. When she took a step back, I mounted and rode to the end of the rope, and led her on to the roundup where Grover heeled her. (Somewhere along before we got to the roundup, we got the extra rope off her when she fell down.)

None of the other boys could come help as they were busy holding the rest of the herd. We finally got the heifers where we wanted them, with no more excitement; except that about 100 head got out on the ice on the river when we were crossing. It held them up, but we got them off and crossed the bridge.

Then Tom Anderson quit today; Tom Sutton yesterday, and Wilson the day before. Grover was some concerned. We cut herd this afternoon.

Feb. 1.

It was warm this morning, 29 degrees above zero! We moved a herd of cows and calves from the South Clover to the North Swamp. I rode Jiggs and didn't see any excitement. It got cold, windy, and snowed for a couple hours.

I rode Chief again this afternoon. I think he would have bucked if he had gotten his head, but I finally talked him out of it. He jumped from under my saddle when I was saddling and almost got away from me. I had him hobbled also.

We moved a herd of cows and calves from Dobkins to the South Clover and opened a field. All the excitement occurred when Don Smith's horse fell and jerked away from him. Herb chased the horse for ¾ of a mile before he caught him in a fence corner,

Feb. 2.

Lots of excitement this morning. We split up the broncs Tom was riding. Dick Reed got Captain. He bucked his saddle off to start with; then tried to jerk away out in the meadow where Dick got off, and jerked Dick flat on his belly. Almost every time Dick got off or went to get on, the horse would try to jerk away.

Cliff Cross got King, and it took Cliff and Grover about half an hour to bridle him. They had to forefoot him; and they still both almost got pawed. He wouldn't line out when Cliff finally got him saddled, and tried to buck a few jumps. Herb got Squirrel. He acted pretty decent all morning.

I got Hopi, the oldest one in the bunch. He's either coming nine or ten years old. This is the third time he's been started. He whirled away as I was 2/3 on him, and went to bucking, but I managed to get set down on him, and get him doubled out of it after 5 or 6 jumps. He was alright except I had to be careful getting off and on the rest of the morning.

Six of us gathered a herd of dry cows in the Red House field, and took them down the river bank to the South Swamp, about six miles as far as I know. It was the first large herd ever taken down along the river. I have taken several small herds along there by myself, and think it is a natural stock way; so suggested to Herb that we take the 7 or 8 hundred dry cows that way, and it worked OK.

This afternoon we turned out some extra horses, and then branded eight new saddle horses. I built the fire. Then after the irons got hot, Herb roped the horses one at a time. I'd bridle them and lead them outside the corral where I hobbled and blindfolded them with my neckerchief. Then Herb put the ZX on them. Most of them stood pretty good, but two or three of them pawed all the air away from where I'd be standing when the iron touched them.

Feb. 3.

Today is Sunday, and this morning we saddled up and rode 6 or seven miles, did about 20 minutes work, and then rode home. We got in about 9:30. The thermometer never registered very far below freezing, but it was one of those mornings when you thought for sure you were freezing to death. Came home after noon, and got the pump primed and the water back on.

Feb. 4.

I rode Hopi again this morning. He never bucked when we first started out. King bucked a little with Cliff. Squirrel, Captain, and Snooker all handled like pretty well-broke colts this morning. We rode to the Coglon where first we powdered two lousy cows. Reed roped one and lost his rope. Spence picked it up and got the cow stopped and jerked down right close to me. Grover stepped off on her and I pitched my rope which he put on her hind legs. They pawed to the one side, and when I went to give a little slack to turn her over, Hopi blowed up. I lost my rope. He only bucked 4 or 5 jumps, but by the time I got back to the cow, Big Don on Spider had the rope. Cliff and someone else caught the other cow. We turned them out, and then rode around to the other corral where a lousy bull was. Grover, on Snooker, roped him by the head. Three or 4 loops were spilled on his heels, and then I got a turn.

Hopi turned his rear to the bull at just the right time, and then I got him turned back and cast my twine in and picked up one hind leg. Hopi bucked a little again when I gave the slack to turn the bull over; but this time I was able to double and spin him to where I could hang on to my rope and flip it over him a couple times as we spun. I got stopped, and we finished the bull.

We ran the 1,300 weaner calves to the Blue Joint field after weighing about 270 of them which averaged 310, and then came home. Didn't work this afternoon; for the Company, that is.

Feb. 5.

I took the truck and went to Red Withers', and picked up a ZX cow that had come down off the rim. She was pretty poor. Looked as if she had been pretty short on feed.

I took Blackie a chunk of beef when I got back, and came home after dinner.

Feb. 6.

Grover, Dick Reed, and I rode to the Coglon. Jim drove the pickup around, and we branded 75 two year old bulls. One of them, we were informed, was a chute fighter; so we were advised to rope him. One more we couldn't hold in the chute, we roped. I caught the first one by the head, and Reed heeled him with his first loop. He roped at the second one (the chute fighter) and missed so I caught him. Reed then throwed several loops before he picked up one heel. I had ridden right up into a corner of the corral, stretching the bull out, and when we gave him slack to turn him loose, he charged me before I could get out of the way. He butted several times at my horse who suddenly became tired of it and kicked Mr. Bull right in the face. The bull then turned and charged the men afoot in the corral and put them all over the fence. I made a dash and opened the gate and let him out.

It was almost sundown when we got back to camp. Grover's and Reed's horses both fell with them during the day.

Feb. 7.

The whole crew rode to the North Swamp where we worked some weaner calves out that had gotten in. Two fellows took the weaners and two more took some bulls elsewhere; and the rest of us rode through the South Swamp and picked up 6 more calves which altogether we took back into the

Square Field and bunched on water, and held them until noon. Came home this afternoon.

Cliff's horse, King, fell with him and jerked away. The boys turned their horses loose and ran them by me as I was unsaddling, and Hopi almost jerked away from me after almost stepping on me.

Feb. 8.

We all started out together, but dropped off in two's and three's at different jobs, that were more to get us out of the bunkhouse than anything else. Finally Dick Reed and I dropped out to ride the Monroe Field. We found a gate knocked down, and a bull on a canal bank where he had no business.

Got in about 10 o'clock. Came home after dinner

Feb. 9.

Didn't work today. Went to Lakeview. Had coffee with Grover. He had brought Bradbury in to pick the crew chuckwagon truck for the second wagon on a 4 wheel drive International.

Feb. 10.

This morning the crew split and half of it moved to the Coglon to do the work of blood testing the cattle for Bangs disease. Cliff, Spence, and Jim (who is also staying at the Coglon) took the men's horses over for them.

We hung around until 11 o'clock waiting for some new saddle horses to show up, but we came home before they did.

This afternoon we moved a herd of about 400 cows and with calves from the Bull field to the North Swamp to get them in line for the Coglon.

Jiggs fell on me and almost broke my ankle.

Feb. 11.

We worked quite a while putting two tight-bag cows back from the North Swamp. They wouldn't go. Sam roped one. Tom Anderson (who came back to work this morning) roped one. Grover and I were both on green broncos. I went with Sam. He went with Tom. I was riding Chief and took quite a while before I could manage him with my rope down; but finally got her heeled, and we got her turned loose.

Tom got fouled in his rope and his cow ran back on him, and he finally had to turn her loose. We got things straightened up though.

The new horses were at the Coglon, and Spence and I took them to the Harris. They were on the run, and we had to go around through two herds of horses. We had quite a fast ride on the thawed ground.

This afternoon we gathered the North Swamp and trailed them only about 3 miles on into the Coglon corrals. Helped he boys work some cattle there and then came home.

Feb. 12.

This morning we gathered the Triangle and took them to the Buck Shack field. Then gathered the bulls from the Coglon field and moved them into the North Swamp.

This afternoon we gathered the Monroe and moved them into the Coglon corrals about 5 or 6 miles. Pulled a dead calf on the way home. Got there just at dark.

Feb. 13.

We rode to the Coglon and worked some cattle and separated some calves and cows. Then worked the bulls out of the herd in the Mule field, and took them to the Triangle.

Afternoon we picked up the first Bangs reactor from the North Swamp, (#474) and took her to the Coglon. We gathered the Buckshack field and put them in the Coglon corrals and worked them.

Grover's and Drew's horses both fell. Got home at dark again.

Feb. 14.

We rode to the Coglon where we helped sort out some cows for a while. Sam and I came to the Cow Camp at noon. We rode through the Bakersfield heifers on the way looking for cows having trouble calving. We rode back to the Coglon after dinner, and helped all afternoon. After sundown we took a herd to the Buckshack field, and then galloped home.

Feb. 15.

Went to the Robinson and Little Robinson fields in the Lower marsh, and picked up a herd and brought them to the Buckshack field (about 15 miles). It was so foggy we could hardly see. I took my coat off while I was on Likely, and he spooked and tried to do something; but I held him up, and he just spun in a tight circle to the left for about 20 revolutions before I could get him stopped. I was getting pretty dizzy. I hung onto my coat and finally got it rolled up and tied behind my saddle while on him.

Tom Anderson's horse fell down twice after noon, and my horse fell once. The sun came out after noon, and thawed the top layer and sure made things slick.

The cattle balled up on us, and wouldn't move; so Grover took his coat off and whipped up some to move them. I decided he needs some help; so I took off my red wool shirt and went to whipping up too. Likely got scared and I went to do something. I went to work on his head with my flopping shirt and then he tried to buck. We hit a slicker spot and his hind feet slipped in under him and down we came. I got my foot up high enough for his hip bone to catch it and he smashed my spur right down so tight that I had to take it off and spread it to wear it home. I got away from him as he was floundering around getting up and he was out of reach before I could pick up my reins. I lost them when we went down, but I kept my red shirt. Spence caught him and brought him back to me.

We got dinner at four o'clock and came home.

Feb. 16.

We went to the Lower Marsh again, and picked up a herd (450 cows), 450 calves. 20 bulls) and brought them to the Mule field (about 12 miles). We met Herb's crew with a herd at The Narrows, coming down to the Lower Marsh. He threw off in a hole and we passed him and held up across the highway where we had a picnic. Barney and Raymond came down in the pickup and brought us a dinner.
It was foggy and cold all morning, and the chuck and coffee shore felt good.

We got our herd into the Mule field about 3 o'clock and then rode to camp. It was cold and foggy all day and I never saw any horses buck or fall.

Feb. 17.

It was to the Lower Marsh again today. We picked up a herd of 469 cows and their calves from the Springfield and put them into the corrals at the Coglon at 2:30 O'clock, (about 13 miles). Herb's crew came from the Coglon, and he helped us today. It made 13 cowboys all told. We had to cross one of Bratton's fields; so we ran the cattle out of the way when we went down through; but when we started back through, they spotted us and came after us on the run. Anderson, and Jim Vance from the Lower Marsh (the 14th man) helped us quite a ways, and I put in about a half hour of pretty wild chousing to turn their cattle and keep them out of ours.

Grover and Herb were both with the lead, so the boys wanted to chouse hell out of the drags; but I finally talked them into taking it easy. It shore did my old eyes good after we had gone a few miles, to ride up along the trail and watch, for almost every cow had her calf with her. We only had about 20 calves without their mothers in the drags when we nooned at 11 o'clock.

We gathered the horses out of the Triangle on the way home and got some more to use. I got Spade back. I've had him turned out for over two months, and I got in a new one, "Whistler."
Sam, Spence, and I brought the change of horses home, and the other boys moved the cavvy to the Harris field.

Feb. 18.

We worked the Bakersfield heifers for heavy ones this morning. We had to pen them up in a fence corner where there was a canal on the third side, in order to hold them, and then they were hell to work out of the herd. Grover finally had to rope two cows and drag them out of the rodero. Anderson heeled them both and I took the ropes off. One got back into the herd and had to be drug out a second time. We brought the cut to the camp corrals for noon, and then took it on to the Dobkins this afternoon.

There was five little calves which we roped out and hauled over in a pickup. Spence caught 4 and I only caught one. I couldn't get Hopi up for a while, and then I let 2 run through my loop. Sam's horse fell on him this afternoon and hurt his ribs, he said, but didn't know how bad. Hopi tried to run off a little. Got home early.

Feb. 19 to Feb. 21.
Moved cattle every day. Sam's horse fell again today.

Feb. 22.
Took a herd of cows and calves to Lower Marsh.
Feb. 23.
Tom and I went to Coglon to help. Got rained out at noon.
Feb. 24.
Fixed blowed-down fence in Harris. Roped two calves from back of pickup.
Feb. 25.
Worked poking ice through " Narrows" weir.
Feb. 26.
Worked on out China Town River Bridge.
Feb. 27.
Went to Lower Marsh for 900 drys.
Feb. 28.
Worked chicken feed horses.

And The Wind Blew

Sitting around the bunkhouse
One cold winter day,
The cowboys were telling lies,
To pass the time away.

Some told of horses they'd rode;
The outlaws they used to tame.
They'd won in the big rodeos,
But this is the first I'd heard their names.

One said he could throw a rope
Like Billy the Kid could shoot a gun.
But the other day catching calves,
I noticed he never got a one.

They knew all the old time outlaws
That had ever left a trail.
I wonder where they met them?
Now it might have been in jail.

I listened to their lying
'Till my ears started to scream.
So I thought me up a whopper!
Boy it sounded like a dream.

I was sitting in a tavern
With this beautiful blonde named Lee.
My heart was all in flutters
For the night she promised me.

  Then a man walked to our table;
  A boxer, six foot three.
  I would have whipped him there,
  But her pleading voice stopped me.

Oh, she was proud of me.
I was so brave and strong.
And we had just got in bed
When Ray rang the breakfast gong!

I Did It Once, So Now I Have To Do It Again

We don't have a TV set out where we live. I doubt very much if one would work even if we had electricity to run it with. We don't live at the end of the trail either, for the desert trails just wander on and on endlessly. If you travel far enough you pass the point where it fades into the sand; and if you know your way around and keep moving on, in time you're back on a beaten path again, and headed for civilization once more.

This is a big desert here. Only a large ranch can survive. Some years there is lots of grass and water. Then there are long dry spells when even the juniper trees on the higher ridges seem to stand around with their tongues hanging out, panting for a breath of fresh moist air.

Every place seems to have humorous descriptive stories, but I believe the one that best illustrates this land on a dry year is the one about the two tourists who were passing through when one of them spied a cow standing off out in the sage brush. He told the other to stop the car. He wanted to go see what the cow was eating.

On returning to the automobile, the driver asked, "Well, did you find out what she was eating?"

"No," was the reply; she had already eaten it."

To run cattle in a country like this, an outfit has to be large. They measure their range in miles and townships instead of acres and sections. Their cattle number by the thousands instead of by the hundreds. Contrary to some opinions, those cattle still have to be handled by "the hired hand ahorseback" or commonly referred to in the northwest as the buckaroo which is the same standing as the cowboy elsewhere. It is beside the point, but I believe the buckaroo takes more personal pride in himself and his horse, and his outfit's appearance than what the cowboys do, However, I may be mistaken as I have only cowboyed in seven states.

    These cow outfits make some awful long hard rides and drives through the springs and summers of some years. Ten or twelve hours, or 40 or 50 miles a day is hard on man and beast. But when you ride 14 to 18 hours and cover from 50 to 70 miles day after day, then you need a crew of tough men and a remuda of tougher horses.
    In some places they break their horses at two and three years old. And get along with them fine. It has its advantages breaking them at that age. Generally speaking, a man doesn't have to be a "Casey Tibbs" (World Champion Saddle Bronc rider

several years ago), to break horses that young. Then they usually make gentle dependable horses and last a full life span if they are not ridden too hard for a few years.

But there aren't any easy short rides out in this country. A horse has to have the age and be ready to pack a man a long ways when the bronco stomper turns him over to the buckaroo crew.

The ideal age to start or break horses out here is from 5 to 7 years old. Then a horse is fully developed or enough so that he can be put right to work without too much danger of being ridden too hard.

Of course this system has some faults too. Sometimes a horse is overlooked or he gets crippled up in the bronco pens, and has to be turned out for a spell. Last year I drew one such horse. He had been gotten up on two previous years to be broken, but both times he had injured himself and had to be turned out again. He was finally turned into the buckaroo crew as a started horse at coming 10 years old. I rode him on the average of about 3 times a week for a couple of months, and in all that time, I only got him away from the bedground one time without him bucking.

That's the main drawback to horses started so old, they just plain hate to give up their freedom, and they usually demonstrate their opinion pretty freely for several years.

One thing about it, this type of horse usually makes a good old horse; but it's usually several years before they are gentle enough that a man will ride them in preference to an older horse, unless he has to.

When the work lets up, a man don't need so many horses in his string to keep in the winter, when it's too dangerous to ride them on the slick frozen ground.

It seems to be quite a problem getting someone who is able and willing to ride this type of horse anymore. When a man does come along that is able to, he usually gets a workout here.

Mostly, the men that will ride cranky horses are the drifting cowboys. Four or five months at the longest are about all they can stay in one place. That doesn't help these horses either, getting a new rider every so often.

I suppose that the drifter would be the category I'd be classed in if anyone cared to class me. I have worked here on the ZX ranch about 10 times in about that many years. I have been here 8 months this time which is about the longest I have ever stayed.

There might be hope for me settling down yet though, as I am just under 30 years old and have a camp which I got by promising the boss I'd try to settle down and stay permanent like in exchange.

I drawed the camp alright, and I also drawed most of a new string of horses last winter when I came back.

Some of them were old horses I knew and liked alright, and some of them were horses I had hoped I'd never have to ride again, for different reasons.

The winter went on pretty well. I got bucked off once early in the fall when my horse got spooked at my rope. I took the most falls of anyone on the crew. It seemed like about every other week there for a while I'd have a horse down, but I managed to get clear of them pretty well. Other than that, it was just the general run of excitement until the bronc stomper quit and we had to take over the bunch of colts he had been working on.

The one I drawed, a sorrel coming 7 years old was the pick of the bunch, or so I thought until I swung astraddle of him. If the old cowboy saying, "It takes a good horse to buck me off, but it don't take him very long," is true, then mine sure must have been quite a pony!

He jumped and kicked at my off spur as I mounted, and then rolled and kicked at my near one by the time I'd picked up the stirrup on the off side.

He bucked just like a Brahma bull rolling and kicking at first one stirrup and then the other. I wasn't just setting up there hoping. I had two hands full of snaffle bit reins, trying my best to jerk his jaw off or his head up or something. The harder I worked on my reins, the more he slung his head and rolled from side to side kicking at my spurs.

As I mentioned, it was in the winter and the corrals were too slick and muddy to be a safe place to be. There were two other boys that had mounted colts just before I'd mounted; so we had all mounted outside. I'd picked the only dry place over toward the ditch bank where I could dry off my boots first. Of course. It had to be right up from the wood pile which we kept to build fires in the morning while waiting for the wrangler to bring in the horses. Then one last warming up if you happened to get saddled up before every one else was ready to go. And, of course, my old pony had to turn and buck right straight through that wood pile, which I saw probably one jump and one fraction of a second before we were right in the middle of it.

That's about how much more time it took for my old colt to roll to the other side and kick at my other foot, and be back out on solid ground again. I thought for sure we would pile up there, but that sorrel never missed a lick. He just used the wood pile for an excuse to be spooked more.

One jump later I was still with him and still had both stirrups (I think), but one jump after that I was on the ground and he was heading for the wild bunch with much haste.

Some of the boys corralled him for me, and after making sure I hadn't been killed, for I had sure taken a beating, I caught him and mounted up again.

One of the boys on a gentle horse helped me this time and we finally got lined out after a few crow hopping jumps which never amounted to much. I did everything I knew of though to prevent a repeat performance, except staying off him.

The second day I rode him we made out fine but the third day he got me again. It was in the afternoon when I saddled up, and the ground was pretty slick from the morning thaw.

He started right in just like he had the first day, rolling and kicking at my feet. I wasn't in too much trouble until about the third jump when he rolled and hit a slick spot and fell, or so I thought he had fallen. Anyhow when I loosened up to try to step away from the wreck, he rolled the other way just like a cat does that is dropped upside down. He kicked and lit on his feet and left me setting there in the mud.

How disgusting! But then there were men around to help me catch him up again. I rode him most every day then for about two months. That is, I would catch him up every afternoon and ride him until he worked up a good sweat, sometimes farther. Some days he pitched a little and sometimes he wouldn't. Finally he got gentle enough that he took his regular place in my string.

Things looked good for me for the summer. I had a good string of horses that I knew and could handle pretty good, and a camp where I could take my wife and family. I wouldn't have to go with the wagon where I'd be gone from home two and three weeks at a time.

Then things got loused up. My little sorrel colt got wire cut just the day before I was ready to head for the summer range. A horse getting wire cut might not sound so drastic to you, and in all probability even in this instant, it's not so bad, but I can't quite convince myself yet.

Getting the horse out to the camp wasn't so much of a problem, even though the 110 miles there, was too far for him to be trailed with my other horses. The boss loaded him on the truck with my camp outfit and hauled him here.

Even then if things had proceeded normally, the cut would have healed in two or three weeks at the most. At the most and at the worst, the horse would have been a little humpy, but after a few days riding he would have settled down again.

Instead, two months have gone by and the cut is just healing up. That isn't a very long time for some, but it's a plenty long time for a seven year old horse which has only been ridden two months to turn bronco again.

It wouldn't be so long at any other time of the year, but right now the grass is at its peak, and even the old gentle horse that my wife rides, wanted to buck one morning a couple weeks ago, when I rode out on him to wrangle my horses.

So here I've been for the last six weeks thinking he looked like he'd be all healed up in about a week, and then I could, or would have to, start riding him again.

Now after sweating him out at about a week at a time, I find that suddenly it is time to cinch my riggin' on and crawl up in his middle again.

That shouldn't worry me so much, for more than likely he'll pitch a little bit for a few saddlings, and then straighten out to the good gentle horse he was coming in to when he got laid up.

Somehow I can't keep worrying though. I am here alone now. My wife went back to Omaha to visit her folks. It's her first visit in quite a while; so she probably won't be back before next month sometime.

The camp tender comes around once a week, but a fellow gets to thinking that would be a long wait if a horse bucked you off and jumped in your middle or got you in some other way.

I know I'm only one of many men in camps throughout the cattle country that have bronco horses to ride, and that all these other men go ahead and ride their horses and do their work, and say nothing of it, but somehow I can't keep from wondering if sometimes when they're out alone, and they have a cranky horse to ride, if they don't get just a little worried too.

I guess there are many such occupations where a man has to shrug his shoulders and put the thought of danger aside, and go ahead and do what has to be done.

So I guess I'll just tuck this little yarn in my chaps pocket and climb up in old Rocket's middle and see if I can't get him headed towards the mail box.

Needless to say, but if you read this, you'll know I've gotten him started once again.

Red Roses

The pale moon was-shining,
From a beautiful star-studded sky.
Two sweethearts were laughing
At the world as it passed by.

A cool breeze was playing
In the boughs of a swaying pine,
To bring the sweethearts together
Like the flowers of a lovely vine.

Their hearts were held together
By the spell of the magic night.
Their love will go on forever,
That they found in the pale moonlight.

Though love has its troubles,
And sometimes, sweethearts must part;
As long as there will be a moon above,
Two lovers shall have one heart.

Over time, the moon is full,
And your sweetheart is far away.
He'll send a bouquet of red roses to you,
And this is what they will say:

"Darling, I am so lonesome tonight.
I know my heart would break in two,
If I couldn't send these roses
With all my love for you.

Letter to Margie

Hi Honey,

    I caught a coyote pup out on the desert yesterday morning. There was a family of coyotes playing in a low place; and they broke and run when they saw me. I ran this pup about a quarter of a mile before I treed him in a sage brush. I got off and caught him and wooled him around a bit; then turned him loose.
    When I got back yesterday, The ZX truck had been here and left us a whole load of block wood - right in the driveway too.
    Some people don't seem to use what brains they've got. The old mother cat had her kittens a couple days ago under the house. I don't know how many or what.

Friday Morning June 20, 1958

Plan on riding my sorrel horse around a bit and then leaving on the bay to ride Mud Lake, Grass Lake and Frederick Butte. Probably be back after noon.
8:30. I've ridden old Rocket and have decided to go wrangle my other saddle horses.
    <u>Gone to the Mail Box.</u>

Saturday Morning June 21
Plan on riding old Rocket and then going down toward Mud and Grass Lakes on Guy. Be back around noon.
Sunday afternoon
I rode Rocket to the mail box this morning. I thought I might get a letter is why I didn't go yesterday afternoon. Thought I'd save the treat for this morning. I got your card Thursday. Guess what I did. Made a cake this morning, I'll tell you I've sorta missed your desserts if you won't make fun of me. Vanilla cake cooked in 3 pie pans. Looks pretty good. Haven't tasted it yet though.

The frosting is still cooling and I've just finished dinner – roast beef, fried sweet spuds, and peas. Bread & coffee. Planned on fruit & cake for dessert later. Got to see about my frosting. Bye.

Monday Morning
It's 8:45. I just got back on Rock and got to the cabin. Guess what? I just barely beat a rain storm here. It's coming down now. I am sending a First Person story. Would you type it up for me and send it on? Cont. on P. 4. And don't change the title or the story or the ending please. And keep your fingers crossed and hope for the best. Also attach my letter to the Editor, to the story; so he'll find it first.

Wish we were together.

Love Red.

The Shining Star

I saw a star, shining in the sky.
I dreamed a dream, I don't know why.
I heard a sound, floating in the air.
I knew a perfume, its fragrance rare.

The star was cold, so far away.
The dream was sad, Oh, how I pay!
Out of a cloud, the sound came clear
The perfume belonged to you, My Dear.

One lonely night, so long ago,
We picked a star, only we two know.
We made our plans 'neath its lonely light.
Though our love is gone, it still shines bright.

At night time in my troubled dreams,
I ride the trails where we shared our scenes.
But I always end in the same old place
Where I bid goodbye to your lovely face.

The birds all sing so beautifully,
Their song of love does torture me.
Their song is the one you used to sing.
Though it pains my heart, to each note I cling.

I took a chance on a summer romance;
Something I shall never do again.
I played the part of a lonely trusting heart;
But I'm glad I invited you then.

You taught me to care, and my love to share;
That Life was really worthwhile.
Your kiss goodnight was a great delight

245

It brought to my dreams, a smile.

To a summer romance, hear the verdict in advance;
With their heart, someone must pay.
They think it's smart, to play with your heart;
But listen and someday you'll hear them say:

Summer romances are fun, but now I'm the lonely, hurt one;
For she loved me and left me all alone.
When she went away, these haunting words did stay:
"Thanks for the summer romance I own."

Listen, my darling, to what I must say.
Please, Honey, before you go your way.
Once I was contented, in a world all my own.

I had no troubles: a life I'd always known.
One day you came along
With your pretty big brown eyes.
I took one look and knew right then
That you were my special prize.

What makes me feel this way?
I've done nothing but mope around all day.
I have no ambition, nor anything more.
I don't even know what I'm looking for.

This morning I awoke; I'm all alone.
I have nothing I can call my own.
I climbed upon a mountain high.
I know the angels heard my cry.

Far across this earth, I've travelled far;
Searching to find just where you are.

Not finding you, I'm living in the past;
Thinking of a love I spent too fast.

They say I've been careless,
My life wasted away.
That I was too fickle:
Why I have nothing today.

They don't know of my mem'ry,
Of days in the past;
When you were my sweetheart.
What a heavenly cast!

I can feel your arms about me;
In my heart you did entwine.
So again I'll say I love you.
A treasure in this mem'ry of mine.

If I never have riches,
Still wealthy, I'll always be.
For I'll have you Darling
In my treasured memory.

Tonight out in a canyon;
There's a cool stream running by;
And high upon a mountain top;
There's a lonesome coyote's cry.

Way out over the prairie,
"Neath the stars sparkling bright;
There moves a sadness in the air;
You know it just isn't right.

The wind is in the trees, whispering
Of a lost tragic romance.
The tall pines are swaying,
For it's their mournful dance.

And there drifts a cowboy
With his head bowed low;
Longing for a pardner
That he misses so.

Will we meet again?
Or will things be the same?
Will she forget me in time?
Or will I forget her name?

The wild flowers that I ride by
With their blossoms proudly held up to the sky,
Give off a fragrance that does compare
With the enticing aroma of your flowing hair.

I'll live and wait with my lonely star.
I'll dream my dream to be where you are.
I'll remember each note that the birds sing.
For our love shall bloom when we're together,
come spring.

What Goes Around, Comes Around

Every time I hear Ian Tyson sing about the MC horses being sold, a tear comes to my eye. It reminds me of Banjo. If you could play a tune on his ribs and hide with your gut hooks when he got melodious, you were quite a hand.

One time when I was with the crew, we were galloping along in double file, going somewhere to work or gather cows, I don't recall which. Anyhow, old Banjo and his rider were even with me. I don't know what spooked him out of a gallop, but he went right straight up in the air, in a high kicking and doubling buck stunt. His feet were right even with my head, and I weren't riding no Shetland pony. Most of those cavvy horses ran from 15 to 17 hands high. It was nip and tuck there for a few jumps, but that old kid on him weren't no beginner. He was dragging cougar tracks off Banjo's shoulders when that horse hit the ground. Three or four galloping, jumping bucks, and Banjo must have decided to wait for another time to play his tune. All in a day's work on a big old cow outfit like the MC.

It don't surprise me at all if ole Banjo took that fellow's trailer apart when he tried to load him up for town! The MC cavvy. I sure hate to think of a good cavvy being split up but I'm sure some of them ended up staying right there in Warner Valley.

When the ranch went bottoms up and was put on the market, I heard a group of the local ranchers went together and made an offer on the MC. When they were to close the deal, they were informed their deal was off. The Audubon or Nature Conservancy or some other ranch-destroying outfit offered more money for the dear old MC. The locals took it to court, and won the case. So, even though it's not the old MC anymore, it is still ranch and cow country. So, again; when I listen to Ian Tyson sing, I think that dear old MC cavvy might have been split up; but Warner Valley is still buckaroo country and holds many fond memories for me.

I knowed the MC way back in the 40's, when Ross Dollarhide, Senior, was the wagon boss. I worked some on the MC and partied every Labor Day week with those buckaroos. Labor Day week was the yearly vacation for all the big ranches in those days.

In '69, I sold my interest in a ranch up at Post, Oregon, and went back to the MC. I was sort of a handyman there. I had my old Freight-liner tractor, a set of double hay trailers, and a double-deck cow "pot." I had three head of horses at the grow-out feedlot, where they ran about 18,000 head. I also had four horses in the wagon crew cavvy. It was a big ranch, and like most big ranches, they did their own butchering weekly; on Wednesday; early evening. Many times when I was available, I'd get a notice to get what help I could find and do the butchering. They had a machinery repair garage and a lumber cabinet shop. If I wasn't busy, I'd be called to help somebody there too.

The ranch ran about 700 herd bulls. Being up north, they were separated from the cattle in the winter. In years past, the bulls were trailed to the desert, dropping off so many at this camp, and the next one, and so on until all the bulls were scattered. This year, they said we'd truck them to the desert; 39, 40, or 41 to a load at each camp.

I hauled all the bulls. You haul bulls as tight as you can pack them without being overcrowded. If they're snug, they don't have room to fight. Hugh Cahill, the cowboss, said he'd have a man to help me load. I replied I didn't need any help; just for them to sort them about 39 head if they were all big; 40 if normal size, and 41 if there were some small ones. To leave a note on each pen where that pen full was to go.

I had a "hot shot" that was a super-duper. It had a Model T Ford coil attached to a 5 foot shovel handle with two one-quarter inch copper wires running down opposite sides and extending about one and one-half or two inches past the end. Those coils were 6 volt, but I had a 12 volt plug in on the back end of my "cow wagon," and a 100 foot cord with a thumb push button up on the handle end. Plugged in, you could hold it in the air, push the button down, and the old blue fire-like lightning would jump back and forth between the points. If two bulls started to fight or become belligerent, I'd hold the business end up over close to their back. If they ignored it, I'd drop the points on their back. If that didn't do the trick, I'd touch them by or under their tail where there was no hair. I have seen it knock two fighting bulls to their bellies. Boy, I'll tell you, they'd hunt for a hole then, to get on or off that trailer.

They had a large set of truck scales there, and I weighed each load just for kicks. Almost every load netted out at 60,000 pounds of bull. And that's a lot of bull.

I finally moved back to my starvation ranch in Colorado. I had to keep trucking as a bull hauler to keep the ghost away. It was in the middle of winter, and I'd picked up a load of cows, way off in the mountains somewhere, that was going to the Salida Sale Yard. I'd hauled in there a lot, so if I got there in the middle of the night, when there was no yardman around, it didn't bother me. I'd unload into an empty pen, put the cow papers in a cubby hole, and be on my way.

On this particular load of old cows, I got there about midnight or later. There was no one around so I opened the gates to a big open pen that had feed and water, and started unloading. On my old pot, for big cows I had four compartments; the rear end which unloaded easy; the top deck, bottom deck and front end. Like I said, the rear compartment unloaded easy, but when I dropped the ramp and opened the gate to the top deck, nothing would budge. I worked and hollered and prodded to no avail. Finally I got my super hotshot out. I couldn't get a hold and do any good hanging on the side of the trailer; so I crawled up on top and laid down flat on my belly. I pulled the dynamite shovel handle through an opening. I had luck. I got the crooked cow lined up, and they started to unload. One stopped in the doorway, so I gave her a boost.

I'm telling you, I really screwed up there. That damn prod pole belched and backfired and kicked me with both hind feet and maybe a front one also! I was sailing through the air and heading downward. I was only about 13 feet off the ground, on top of the trailer, but I felt like I was lifted another 2 or 3 feet before I started shooting toward old Mother Firma. Like I said, it was the middle of winter at Salida, Colorado. There was two or more feet of heavy slushy snow squashed out to the side of the trailer from backing up to the chute.

Somehow I managed to flip over and come down back first. When I hit that snow pile, there was a big swooshing sound, and snow flew every direction. I squashed that spot right to the bare frozen ground before I stopped my descent towards Hades. Glory be! I wasn't hurt a bit! I just shook myself like a good horse would; crawled back up to the top of that trailer again, and got unloaded. But I'll tell you, I shore was careful with that thunder stick after that!

Mountain Meadow

I went to work for Louis Draper in the spring of '57. He said, "I'll put you on the payroll now and move you up to Mountain Meadow Camp in two or three days, or if you want to wait until you get up there, you can start then."

I needed a job bad so I said. "I'd just as soon go on the books right now."

He signed me up and says, "Check with me in a day or two, and we'll move up there."

The first night, it clouded up. The next morning, when I looked out the window of our cabin in Babcock Hole, there was three feet of snow on the level. I have never seen anything like it before or since. It snowed all night without a breath of wind, letting the flakes all fall straight down.

I had an old '31 Model A Ford pickup that we used to get in and out of 'The Hole.' The snow on the ground was level with the top of the Model A's fenders. Here sat the outline of an old pickup, three feet high above the snow surrounding it. The hood, lights, cab, and "rumble seat" were all corresponding heights.

About mid-morning, the sky cleared up, the sun came out, and the level of the snow dropped one foot. Shortly after noon, it clouded up again, and snowed another foot. This was in May.

At a lodge below Mountain Meadow, it snowed 12 feet. Consequently, it was the first of June before enough snow melted for us to move up to Mountain Meadow.

Mountain Meadow Camp sat at 9,500 feet. I think it's still up there in the clouds, if the mountain hasn't settled any. We finally moved up there the first part of June with a month's wages in our pocket to live on. You should see that country in the spring after a good wet winter. Columbines and lupine everywhere, wild rhubarb at a very old deserted homestead, fish in all the streams, and water everywhere. The grass was stirrup high.

Punching cows in that high steep country is a lot different than down on the flats or in rolling hills. Cattle learn pretty quick that they can outrun you if they head downhill. When they hit the bottom of a draw, they can head right back up the steepest slope and beat you to the top.

Mostly in that high country, when you're riding and spot cattle, you ease toward them real slow. When they see you and raise their heads, you hold up and keep quiet until they go to grazing again. You might have to repeat this several times before you can get up to them and move them off slow.

We were gathering some cows in country that topped out a little below 11,600 feet at Deer Peak. I had been sent up on this left-hand ridge which was a little lower than where the rest of the crew was heading.

I'd just got up on the ridge when I came around the timber into an open meadow where 20 or so cattle were grazing. I was into them and above them before we saw each other, and I was probably as startled as the cattle were. They sold out in a hard run down country. I immediately thought that there wouldn't be any of the crew where they'd hit the valley to catch them. I knew the country well enough to know that if I rode hard on past where the cattle were, I could probably beat them to the slope on the other side of the draw above them, and would maybe be able to catch them.

I turned down the first open deer trail I came to, and was dropping right down the grade when I saw a barbed wire that some bygone nesters had strung through the trees. It was right in front of us and about two feet off the ground.

My horse saw it too and tried to jump it, but we were coming on it too fast. He sure got fore-footed. I don't know how far we travelled through the air. I'd jerked my feet free of the stirrups and tried to get away from him, but about that time, we hit the ground and skidded sideways down the hill.

Somehow, the fall had thrown me right smack dab back in the saddle. My horse's head, neck, and rump slammed into two or three trees with my body in the saddle sitting upright, but with only my upper half pointing downhill. My right leg was all the way under him.

I thought my horse had broken his neck. His eyes were all milky and glazed over. A whale of a fix!

Under a dead horse in the timber where the crew might or might not find me. I finally got my left boot off and got out of the left leg of my pants. Then I got my left foot up in the seat of my saddle and drug my right leg out from under the horse, bootless and pantless. I also left my long johns under the horse. I had peeled some hide off, but it sure felt good to get that unbroken leg out from under that horse.

About that time, the horse started coming around, but he couldn't do anything but paw the air with all four feet because he was lying with them pointed uphill.

I decided maybe I could get my lass' rope on a hind foot and get him worked around to where he'd be able to get up, but I couldn't get my rope out from under him.

I'd been riding him in a hackamore with hair reins and a great long McCarty. I got one end of it around one of his hooves and heaved. I was barefooted and didn't have nothing on but my shirt and my hat. Between me pullin' and him strugglin', I got him flipped around with his head pointed downhill and all four feet under him.

He jerked my McCarty out of my hands and hit a run, but he got fouled up in the timber, and I was able to get him stopped. I finally got all my clothes back on and rode gently on down into the valley. The crew was there with my cattle and quite a bunch of their own. They were just getting ready to come hunt for me when I showed up.

I told them what had happened and then finished by saying, "It would have been interesting if I'd been riding old Nelly and they'd caught me chasing her down through the timber half naked. "
It was good for a laugh!

When I'd first arrived at the Mountain Meadow Camp, they'd sent an older cowboy up with a big truckload of horses for us to use. It was easy to see they hadn't been used for a while, with the witch knots in their manes and tails and long feet. I suggested to Harry that we should get them up and give them a little manicure.

Harry knew the horses. This one was this way and that one another type; and that big rawboned sorrel gelding that was chewing and kicking anything close, was Old Cougar. He was pretty much an outlaw and didn't get used much.

When I walked into the corral, here he was eating and kicking; so I roped him first. I intended just to put him in a separate corral to protect the other horses.

"You're not going to saddle him?" he asked, worried.

"No, Harry, I'm just getting him out of the way, but if I was younger I'd ride him right now." By the time I got to the gate, I decided.

"Hell, I ain't that old."

I wasn't but about 28 then, and that would be a good time to try him out. I kicked him in the belly, threw my bridle on, and grabbed my saddle and slung it on him as hard as I could. I cinched him up tight and never even untracked him. I kicked him in the belly again, gathered him up close, and slid up into his middle.

I had a snaffle bit with a long set of heavy split reins. When I got up in his middle, I did several things all at the same time. I squalled like a panther as loud as I could, brought the loose ends of those heavy reins down hard under his belly, just in front of his hind legs, and drove my spurs as hard as I could in his shoulders.

Unbelievably, we left in a good high gallop for a half hour or so, with no buck.

I wouldn't have been so smart if I hadn't out-figured him. He was 12 to 18 years old, with old saddle marks. They said he was a good horse if you could ride him. I gambled that back in his past, he'd had a waddy or two that had fit some hellish rides on him, and if I acted like I was going to eat him up, maybe he'd think I was one of those old timers from out of his past.

I never did tell anyone this for a long time, but whenever I planned on riding him the next day, I'd pick a fight with my wife the evening before. That way I'd be mad enough to thump him around and bluff him out again. I used him a lot and he only bucked with me one time. I was using him to pack salt; three blocks cinched down tight on each side, which weighed 300 pounds. I was leading him. He got peeved at something and jumped and kicked at my head. He hit the ground bucking. I had my hands full with my horse, but I was able to hang on to Cougar. It only took about a quarter mile to scatter that salt. That part of the pasture got salted good. I didn't go back and pick it up.

All In A Day's Work

Long years ago when I was a young man, I worked on several outfits in northern Nevada and southeastern Oregon, so I have many colorful yarns about those times. I was in the last draft of World War II, (too young before that), because I was out with a chuckwagon cowboy crew and missed my call. We didn't get any mail after we left headquarters in the spring until late fall, unless someone might bring something up where we were 150 miles up in the mountains.

When Korea came along, I was laid up from a bad horse wreck so was Classified 4F, so missed it, to my relief. I worked on big outfits of 20,000 head of cattle or more for years. Worked in Montana, Wyoming, Colorado, New Mexico, California, Arizona, and both Nevada and Oregon.

 I get a kick out of the association of being like "30 day Bill." He was known as that because he seldom worked for any outfit more than 30 days at a time. Sometimes he'd stay longer. He was a good hand.

We were all in the same class as "30 day Bill". We moved from wagon to wagon. If we never quit, leaving them in a pinch; when we came back, they'd put us on if they were short handed.

Now, I'm in my 90's. However, way back in the 1940's, I was sitting in a truck stop in Colorado, not eavesdropping, but just listening to some cowboy sort of looking fellers in the next booth. One says," Well, if you want to see or work on some real old time chuckwagon ranches, you should go out to northern Nevada; Elko, Wells, or Winnemucca, or eastern Oregon. There's ranches there that run twenty to twenty-five thousand head. They still do the cowboying in the same old ways.

All of my buddies and relatives were getting killed in World War II, and I would be subject to get called in the draft in another birthday or two. "To Hell with it!" I quit high school as a sophomore and headed west in my old "29" Chevy coupe. I was going to have some thrill out of life before I got my thrills as a war casualty. I worked on the big outfits like that cowboy truck driver mentioned, for many years. In the north, the chuckwagons pulled out about the middle of March, and tried to make it back in by Thanksgiving Day. It was a great life!

People ask me why I don't write more about those old days. I have written a number of accounts, and toned them down from actual happenings. Nobody will believe them. They think I made them up; or just stretched the truth. On one outfit, I had over 250 sections (a section is a square mile) of range to watch over. I came in at night, and checked my BLM map of the area from point to point where I had ridden that day. Of course, I had ten head of big "ole stout ex-rough string broncs" in my string. One of them, a new horse they'd given me, I was riding close to sundown. I had to go through a drift fence gate about five miles from camp. I mentally calculated where I'd ridden and figured I put about 80 miles on old Custer that day. It was only about five miles to my camp; so I thought I'll take it easy on him. About a hundred yards further, a jackrabbit jumped out from under the nose of my horse. He went to bucking and almost got me, before I got him lined out in a gallop!

I remember thinking afterwards, "You sorry old bastard, I've only put almost 100 miles on you today. Now here you're trying to buck me off." All right. We were heading toward camp, and when he quit bucking, and lit galloping, I just galloped him the short five miles on into camp. He didn't falter and was ready nine days later (his regular turn) to make another circle.

I had a camp and some corrals, but no place to keep ten head of horses. My wrangle pasture had only 26 sections in it. I'd ride the nine horses, turning out the one each night when I came home, that I'd ridden that day. When I got down to the tenth horse, I'd use him for a wrangle horse. Sometimes it would take me three days to find my extra horses again and get them corralled; so I could start another round of my desert tours.

I didn't do much as far as handling cattle was concerned, but I skylined myself as much as possible, and left fresh horse tracks at the water holes to warn the little nesters that were high-grading calves to be on the lookout. I've seen more than one pickup and horse trailer scoot across the desert when I skylined myself. They were slick-earing, once, when they saw me ahorseback. They knew it was time to get out of the area. They knew if I caught them, they'd go to jail.

I was still about sixty-five head short and was scouting the country for where they were. Frederick

Butte stood up high in one corner of the area. I seldom carried a lunch, but this one day I had a sandwich rolled up and tied behind me on my saddle. I decided, after several hours riding, I'd ride up to the top of the Butte, eat my sandwich, and study the country where to look for the cattle. When I got to the top of Frederick Butte and circled around to find the spot to rest and eat; off to the west five or six miles I could see a string of cattle moving into the juniper country. I knew there was a lot of good grazing, spread out over that way. My thoughts were I'd better head that way before they got scattered out and I'd miss some of them.

Down off the Butte we came, and hitting a slow lope for a mile or more, I remembered I'd not eaten the sandwich I brought that morning. I reached behind me and got it untied without spilling it, and started to eat. As I said, I was in a slow lope. Dempsey, my dog, (he was a Boxer) was pacing me along, by my horse's right shoulder, looking up at me, as I munched my sandwich. All year, when Dempsey rode with me, if I had anything to eat or drink, he got half of it. He kept eyeballing me, wanting to know when I was going to give him his share. I'd finished my half, and had the last half held in my hand. I dropped my hand down by my knee. Looking at Dempsey I said, "Well, if you want it, jump up here and get it."

I had got Dempsey as a weaner pup. I think he knew English better than I did. I hadn't quite finished telling him that, than he hit the ground, leaped with his front feet against my horse's neck and his rear feet on his flank; snatched the sandwich out of my hand, and was back galloping beside me, eating his half.

I think my caballo thought a mountain lion had jumped up and hit him on the shoulder, and he was determined to get rid of it. He damn near bucked me off, as hard as we were traveling, before I got him settled back down to a good gallop.

We found our cattle and got them gathered and trailed eight or ten miles on into camp. Me and my dog gathered 2,226 head of cattle off 48 sections of pasture in two weeks. I had found four carcasses that summer; so I was only two head short of what was counted into that little pasture in March.

All in the day's work.

SECTION III

- The Later Years 1970's-2000's
- The Southwest
- Horses, Stagecoaches, Movies

Application For A Job

Dear Sir,

A very valuable asset, besides understanding budgeting and cost controlling, for a manager of a large ranch, might be a working knowledge of the ranch, and personal experience in all phases of the ranching industry, and especially all the phases of it that are connected with a ranch like the ZX.

Ranching has changed to the extent that a diversified business experience would be a real asset. The trucking industry plays a large role in today's ranching, and knowing it would help cut hauling costs.

Today, the ranch manager must be able to meet and discuss budget along with the public; what with the BLM, the Forest Service, and sportsmen's clubs and timber claims that are accessing the ranches increasingly. In a business where you have to deal directly with the public as individuals and in large groups, a manager must be able to work out the problems of joint occupancy of such areas with diplomacy. The desirable end result is that everybody gains a little and nobody loses a lot.

A new manager needs to have a good working knowledge of the ranch and the area, but have no obligations or demanding ties in the community. This would certainly be a step ahead. It might take a year or two for a total outsider to understand the ways and the "why's" of a ranch, the size of the ZX.

All businesses run by superintendents must be planned, budgeted, and controlled. For the past 18 years, I have been in private business, such as ranching, trucking, tourists, and show business. To go back to the start:

In 1944, at the age of 15, I left Colorado and ventured out to Paisley, Oregon, where I got hired on at the ZX, breaking mules to drive in the hay fields there. After haying, I quit the ranch and went to work with the cowboy crew. For several years, I drifted from the wagon crew to the hay crew. I liked to work with those mules. I worked for several other large ranches across the West.

In 1953, I returned to Colorado and talked my way into Pueblo Junior College where I studied veterinary medicine for two years. I graduated but wasn't admitted to Fort Collins, because they said it was impossible to work your way through school there. A person needed all the extra time to study, to make it, and I didn't have the necessary funds without working.

In 1956 I returned to the ZX where I stayed pretty steady until the summer of 1961. I had gotten married in 1954, and had two little girls, Holly and Tammie, by that time. That summer, I got the idea to buy a small ranch near Bend, Oregon; so quit the ZX and moved. Learned flood irrigation!

The years I spent on the ZX, I guess I must have done, or helped do every job there was except work in the office. Basically I cowboyed while there, but I was one of those guys that could do other things besides ride a horse, so I was quite often the one called out in a pinch to come fix something or to go help somebody.

I knew the ZX and how it functioned from the inside up. Since leaving there, I've broadened my experiences and been personally involved in almost every facet of ranching possible.

Early in 1963, two lawyers and I formed a corporation, and bought a good sized, run down ranch at Post, Oregon, which I managed and ran until 1969. There I was exposed to all the problems of a large ranch, only on a smaller manner, but much more personal. Worn out machinery to be fixed, irrigation ditches which I learned to survey and rebuild so the water could be used to raise hay and improve the pastures. Buy cheap but good young cows and build up a herd, and have to use our partner's sons for hired help, and provide dude ranch entertainment for the pleasure of the lawyers' families on summers and holidays, with my wife doing all the cooking for no pay. We did all the work and built up the ranch and the cattle herd. They used it for a tax write off and cheap vacations for their kids.

By 1969, we'd had enough, and we sold our share of the ranch to a new partner, and moved to the MC Ranch at Adel, Oregon. I leased my diesel truck to them. I spent the next year dividing my time between trucking, doctoring cattle, castrating, plumbing, carpentry; just as a jack of all trades, including mechanics and welding.

In 1970 we moved back to our own small ranch in Colorado. We had a small herd of registered Shorthorn cows and registered Morgan horses. I started up a hay business and ran two trucks hauling hay and steel for several years.

In our "spare" time, I started breaking our 15 horses to drive. In the winter of '75, we ordered a new "Abbott-Downing" stagecoach to be built to original specifications. Our coach wasn't ready on time, so John Frizzell who was making it, brought us one he had just finished repairing for someone else that we could use until ours was finished.

We hauled it and our horses to St. Joseph, Missouri, and on May 28, 1976, we began our stagecoach trip from there and arrived in
Sacramento, California 100 days later, exactly as we had planned. That trip took lots of planning and budgeting. It took two years of paper work, and corresponding with the 140 towns enroute, to schedule the trip and to get everybody's approval connected. We had every day's event planned out up to a year in advance of the trip. It mostly worked right out to the dot.

    In January of '77, we were invited to bring our coach and six horse hitch to Washington D.C. as a representative of the "17 western states" for President Carter's Inaugural Parade.   That was an event of a lifetime we enjoyed.

    Later that year we set up a stagecoach tourist business in Colorado, and were doing quite well, until Monty Montana Jr. talked us into joining his Buffalo Bill's Wild West Show. We showed in Louisville, Kentucky, then New York City.

He was a good showman, but a poor business man. The show went broke in New York, so we loaded up and went back to Colorado. Unloaded coach and horses. Packed a couple bags and found a place in Arizona. Moved to Apacheland and set up our tourist business there.

After a while, I became the manager there. When the owners of the town decided to go more to "disco" entertainment, we decided to give it up, as we preferred our "Old West" type.

The time spent stagecoaching was a real education in human relationships. As town manager, I was subjected to all types of pressure with employees, shop keepers, salesmen, and entertainers; not to mention the tourists, and the budgeting, and planning the show business; meeting the public and speaking to groups. We are here living on a friend's ranch, with no permanent commitments.

With my experience in life and ranching, private business, and handling people, I feel I could run the ZX as good or better than any of the managers I've known there in the past 30 years. Most of the old timers I knew around Paisley have died, but I knew both Tom and Paul Brattain quite well, for as many years as I've known the ZX.

Judge Dick Hoppes of Prineville, Oregon, has known me for many years, and he would certainly be willing to sit down and discuss the situation with you, if you feel you might be interested in me.

U.S. District Court Judge Ted Goodwin was ranch raised up in the Paulina country, and I've known him quite a few years.

Jack Thompson owns and operates a large trucking outfit in Pueblo, Colorado. I've known and worked with and for him for several years.

As just a cowboy, I worked on the ZX from 1946 to 1961. I hope this experience qualifies me to be your ranch manager.

Adios,

Red Cloud Wolverton

The Inaugural Parade

The night we received word that we had been invited to bring our stagecoach and six horse hitch to Washington D.C for the parade, my wife and I lay awake most of the night with excited anticipation, thinking and discussing the coming event. It all came about so unexpectedly, we could hardly believe it.

That evening of January 6th, we'd plowed out through two to three feet of snow from "Babcock Hole," the name of our ranch home high up in the mountains of Colorado, to visit our neighboring ranches about some stagecoaching plans we had made. By the time we got back in to our ranch, we were in high spirits from discussing our future plans.

When we got home, our kids told us that Jack Thompson and Sherman Boulter had borrowed a four wheel drive rig to come tell us that we'd been invited and that we were going to the Inaugural Parade. That made too much excitement for us to be able to settle down.

Bright and early the next morning, we hot-footed it right in to Jack's office in Pueblo, Colorado, to get the facts. He had a trucking and freighting business. We still couldn't believe it, but sure enough, "Yes, the parade chairman for the equestrian division of the Inaugural Parade had phoned Jack's office the day before, hunting for us to invite us to the parade."

At first, she just asked how she could get a hold of me. She sounded so disappointed when Jack told her that at that time of year, the easiest and surest way was to load a saddle horse in your pickup, head up into the mountains, drive as far as you could; then unload the horse and ride the rest of the way. Jack persuaded her to tell him why she wanted me.

Jack had spent so much time and effort with our stagecoach ventures that he told her we'd be thrilled to come to the parade, and that he would get word to us that night; and that she'd hear from us the next day. Jack and I spent most of the morning on the phone talking to Nancy Green, the parade chairman, covering the details of planning the trip and the parade event.

We decided right away to take at least 12 horses with us; the six horse hitch and six head of outrider horses. Since it is about 2,000 miles from Pueblo to D.C., we decided we'd better allow at least four days travel time to get back there. The parade was scheduled for the 20th, but at least one of us had to be there on the 19th for our official parade entry, in order to show in it. To be on the safe side, since winter was coming on fast and furious, we planned to leave Pueblo on the 14th.

The horses had to have a 6 month Coggins test and health certificate in order to be able to be stabled at the race track, where they wanted us to stay. It had been about nine months since our last Coggins test. It takes about a week to get the results so we had to start moving. A bigger problem than the Coggins test was that we'd pulled their shoes and turned our horses out in the mountains when we came back from the National Morgan Horse Show in November.

It was the middle of a tough, cold, snowy winter. I had no idea what the parade street might look like; so I figured I'd best be prepared for the worst. I thought rubber shoes for all the horses would be the answer. When I checked them out, I found the cost of rubber horseshoes was about $14.00 per hoof. I decided to try something else.

I went to a large tire repair shop to see if I could find something that I had in mind. There I found a light 2 ply nylon car tire with a mud and snow tread. There was what looked good to me in a blowed out almost new tire. The whole surface was in smaller than ½ inch squares with the grooves both crossways and length ways. It looked good. I decided to shoe Max Brand, a large half Morgan horse that belonged to our daughter, Tammie. I cut a piece of the surface in a size larger than Max's hoof and nailed it on. The first shoe problem was that when the shoeing nail went through the tire, it changed the angle when it reached the hoof; so I had to drive the nail at the proper angle to have it reach the hoof at the right angle. It worked. So, after getting the rubber nailed and clinched, I set the hoof down on a heavy board. Then I took a sharp wood chisel, and with a hammer, trimmed the rubber to fit the nailed on hoof.

After getting all four hooves finished, I decided to try Max out. The streets in Pueblo at that time all had about two inches of hard frozen icy snow pounded on them. The sun had come out quite warm for the winter time; so were very slick. I rode Max at a walk first and stopped him quick. No slipping. So I rode him in a good trot on that slick snowy street. No problem. Next I put him in a good gallop and set him up easily. Those rubber shoes on that road were almost like riding on iron shoes in the dirt. I made and shod 14 head of horses, or 56 feet, with my home made rubber shoes, that only cost the price of the nails and my labor.

 Every parade presents some new kind of a problem. D.C. would be no exception with the cold winter weather moving in, causing icy streets and slick pavements. Our horses are very well broke to drive and handle good, but they do have lots of "go" in them. I just won't take them to a parade unless I have worked them enough to be sure they are settled to handle the way I want them to do.

 I had to get these guys out and drive them every day for a week to make sure I could stand the cold, and be able to handle them in it. I drove them for several days in Pueblo, before leaving for D.C. We even made a practice run, as a dress rehearsal, up Main Street in Pueblo, with a full load of dignitaries to help condition the horses to the city ways.

Out in the mountains or on the desert in the cold weather wouldn't be so bad. A fellow could bundle up and even drive with mittens on, but in a parade in a strange town you need to be very alert, with a foot on the brake lever and finger gloves on your hands. I don't know of anything that can be as cold as two fists full of lines, on a 20 degrees below zero day. Each of those days driving in Pueblo, I became more accustomed to the cold, and figured out how to get on more clothes and how to hang an old kerosene lantern under my seat to get a little heat on my hands, from the mantle. By the time the 20th would get there, I was sure I could take whatever Mother Nature saw fit to dish out.

How we were going to move to D.C. was a big problem, we started working on right away. We have a 40 foot "pot" trailer we've converted to a horse van; so we had plenty of room for all our horses, tack, hay, and grain. Jack had a brand new diesel tractor which hadn't even been out on the road yet. He volunteered it to pull our horse van. The only problem was, it was a very long wheel base, and most of the eastern states won't allow that long of a rig. Then, wouldn't you know, our problem proved to be a blessing in disguise!

We were finally able to route the trip down through Missouri, across Kentucky, West Virginia; then Virginia, and up through Maryland. We hit some 20 degree below zero weather going across Kentucky, but that was good in comparison to what they were having up across the northern route we had originally planned on.

Next, we were faced with who all were going with us. We just couldn't see going to the D.C. parade without taking both our families with us, even if it meant taking four kids out of grade school, and two out of college to do it. I asked our 18 year old daughter, Tammie, "Are you going to start college or go with us?" It didn't take her long to answer, "You better believe it that I'm going to D.C.!" Jack's son, Keith, also dropped out of college to make the trip with us. Tammie immediately invited her friend, Julie Gray, our neighbor's daughter, the Queen of our local Florence Saddle Club, to go with us. When she asked her high school teachers what they thought, they replied. "Take off two weeks and go, by all means,"

Joe Herin, my relief driver on our stagecoach trip last summer, had moved back to his home bed grounds of Prineville, Oregon. I wanted him, and he sure deserved the right to be up in the shotgun seat of that coach in the parade. It took a while for him to make up his mind, but when he found out my brother, Tom Wolverton, a neighboring cowboy rancher was going to fly back to D.C. to fill in as an outrider for us, Joe couldn't resist any longer. Joe and Pearl Herin and Tom and Beverly Wolverton flew to D.C.

Jack had a large motor home which just gave us half enough traveling room from Pueblo; so Jack rented a motorhome for us to drive back there. Jack pulled the stagecoach on its trailer behind his camper. We had a small U-Haul type of covered trailer behind ours which was full of suitcases and hatboxes. Everybody had to take along a new hat to wear in the parade. Sherman would drive the new truck, and when we got to Kansas City, he'd pick up Charlie Johnson, his wife, and his horse. Charlie could help drive the truck and be an outrider in the parade, a position he certainly was entitled to as he had ridden quite a ways with us on our trip last summer. When I brought our horses to town to get ready for the parade, I had brought one extra. You never know when something can happen to put a horse out of commission for a few days. The extra horse I brought is sure enough a good dependable traveler, but he does have a nervous nature; so isn't the ideal parade type. I didn't want to use him unless we had to, but as it turned out, it was lucky we had brought him.

A few days after we'd gotten the invitation, there was a phone call in at Jack's office for me. It was Miss Almabeth Carroll, Miss Rodeo Colorado 1977, on the line. She said she had been invited to come to D.C. by our Congress man, Evans, for the event. She had gone to Denver and met the people, whom she didn't especially care to go with as she would be riding in a car full of people. She wondered if it might be possible for her to ride with us in the parade.

I sure am soft hearted, especially when it comes to being handled by the pretty girls; so, of course I answered it would be fine with me; but I guess I'd better check in with the officials in D.C., and I'd call her back. There was no problem, so when I returned her call, I told her that we'd be delighted to have her; and that I had a horse she could ride. However, she would have to take second position to our daughter, Tammie, in leading our entry. Tammie had worked all summer and led our stagecoach through many parades; so I figured she was entitled to lead it in this parade.

Almabeth is a very nice person. She answered that any spot I had for her would be fine, or she would even be pleased to ride inside the coach. Since she came along with us, I took my trusty near wheeler horse, Bandito, out of the hitch and gave him to her to ride. Romal, the extra horse had to replace Bandito in that near wheeler position in the 6 up.

We arrived in D.C. early enough to be able to drive on the afternoon of the 18th and the morning of the 19th. There were about 300 horses in the parade, most of which were stabled at the Rosecroft Raceway stables. That's about 10 miles from downtown D.C. The military police was to escort us into the staging area that morning of the 20th in two waves. The first was to be in line ready to leave the racetrack at 8:15 A.M. We were in that group. We all had designated spots in the staging area where we were to unload our coach and horses and hook up. Then the camper pulling the coach trailer, and our big horse van had to be moved across town to the area at the end of the parade where we could reload.

After the stagecoach was hooked up, we had to drive about a block to the assembly area where we waited to go into the parade line up, as it was in progress ahead of us. We had to move from our unloading area as the second wave of horses were to use the same area to unload in. We had lots of good help, and I had our unloading and hooking up blueprints all laid out in my head. It worked out best to call out what needed to be done, if the extra help didn't already know, rather than to try to tell them all what steps to take, and in what order beforehand.

I was approached by a man packing a large TV camera. He asked me for a quick rundown on our unloading, harnessing, and hooking up procedures; but after laying it out for him, I was too busy for a while to ever notice what shots he took. We were allowed ½ hour to unload, hook up, and move out. I think we used two or three minutes extra, but we were out of the way before the next wave of horses moved in. Here it was about 10:30 AM, all harnessed, saddled, hooked up, and ready to dance but no place to go. Our horses are an active bunch, and are used to being driven hard after they are hooked up, not standing and waiting for three long hard cold hours. Those are the disagreeable honors of being in a parade. The actual parade might move like clockwork, as each different entry is fed into its line; but the entries still lined up waiting, sometimes have a long wait.

We all enjoyed the morning even though the wind was a little cool. We got to see quite a few of the other entries, and, of course, quite a few people came by to look our outfit over. There were even a "few" pictures taken while we waited.

Our first thrill and excitement occurred as we had to pass a large float whose outside was a complete shell of plate glass mirrors. Our horses have seen their reflections in lots of store windows as we passed by, and I didn't think this would bother them; but it sure did! That stagecoach and six horse hitch coming right straight at them almost caused all our horses to stampede and head the other way!

The lead team doubled clear back almost beside the swing team, before one of our outriders moved in fast, and I was pulling in hard on the lines, and we were able to stop them. It was a little scary! We no sooner got that straightened out and on by that spooky outfit than we ran into another monster! There sat an old time steam engine painted in bright green, with red and black trim. It was just a-chuggin' and a-huffing and a-puffing, and sure looked suspicious. I hauled in all the slack I could get out of the lines, and got a new perch on the brake lever with my foot. I was prepared none too soon, for about that time, with a loud hissing roar, it shot a tremendous greenish white cloud of steam bellowing right out toward the broadside of my lead team! I shot the brake lever full forward, and hauled in on those lines with a good stout steady pull and was able to hold my horses on the pavement in a beautiful ballroom dance. Luckily for us, we were able to move on ahead and fall right into our position in the parade and to continue on going.

    We had brought some sandwiches and coffee and soda pop along in the coach with us, so the waiting wasn't nearly as bad as it might have been. The parade started right on schedule. Finally at about 1:30 PM, we started moving up. The jigsaw puzzle pieces of the parade were fitted together, and we headed down Pennsylvania Avenue. We made the parade with our three queens side by side, leading us, with Tammie in the center, Julie Gray on the left, and Almabeth on the right. Next rode our 10-year old daughter Wendy, and Keith; then came the six horse hitch of matched chestnut Morgan horses pulling our 12 passenger stagecoach.

    Brother Tom rode the left flank close to the near wheeler. Charlie rode the right flank, close to the off wheeler. We had six passengers in the coach— Margie, Beverly Wolverton, Geneva (Jack's wife), Renae Thompson, June Johnson, and John Carroll. There was quite a motley crew on top. I was driving. Joe rode shotgun beside me. Jack, with his coonskin cap, was behind Joe. Sherman and John Thompson had taken our equipment, parked it, and made it back in time to climb to the coach top. Jack's boys, Eddie and Dicky, and our son, Kip, sat on the bedroll on top. Bob Zanes and John Thompson were on the top seat over the back boot of the coach.

I had an old time long haired black bear coat pulled on over my down filled coat. Joe and I also had a large cape type buffalo robe pulled over our legs. I actually was pretty warm most of the time. Also had that kerosene lantern hanging under my seat that made quite a difference too, especially keeping my hands warm to handle the lines.

The first turn to the left as we fell into position was a little "raggy", as far as a perfectly performed maneuver was concerned, due to the horses still being quite chargy, but I doubt if anybody but Joe and I noticed it. The parade regulations demanded that we keep right up close to the entry ahead of us. Our outrider queens did a good job of staying exactly where they should be. I fudged every chance I got, giving myself more room behind the queens; so that several times when the band ahead of us had to stop, I could pull the coach horses down to a slow walk, and just before I'd crowd the queens too hard, they'd get to moving again. I only remember having to stop three times in the entire route.

That hitch we had in D.C. is very responsive and really starts good. I've taught them to start on a whistle command from me, which works real good in noisy parades. They can usually hear it above all other sounds, but the D.C. parade was the loudest one I've ever been in. The sounds from the P.A. systems really blasted out, and they had so many sets that the sounds from each two sets over lapped each other. One of the times when we stopped, the noise was so bad, my lead horse couldn't hear my whistle, but the swing horses and wheelers must have; as they started to step out. I was holding all the horses fairly snug, so when the leaders didn't start, I jingled Romeo's line. He raised his head and half looked back down toward the coach. When he saw the other horses starting to move, he swung right into step and Rebel went with him. I was more cautious after that, when I had to stop, and I didn't have any more starting problems.

Tom's horse, Buddy, a big tall Morgan got quite nervous during the parade, and put on quite a show for the spectators along the route. I think he traveled further backwards and sideways than forwards. Tom let on like it embarrassed him to have his horse put on such a show, but confidentially I think I saw Tom spurring him a time or two, and I'm sure he liked it. This was next to Romal. He did real good for about the first half of the parade. Finally his nerves got the best of him. From then on, through the rest of the parade, about every block he'd have a fit of nervous 'uncoordination'. He'd drop his head as much as he could and try to buck the harness off. The only way I could talk him out of it was to throw him the slack on his line and whack him on the rump at the same time. Now that doesn't sound so difficult; but to be able to do that while you're holding five other horses to a dancing walk, that would like nothing better than to hit a high trot or a good swinging gallop, creates two fists full of problems.

It was the most difficult parade to handle the hitch in, of any parade I have ever driven in. I was about as busy as a man could be. I told Joe and Jack and Sherman that they'd have to do the waving back. I think they must have responded as I think they all had stiff arms the next day. I seldom had time to look or wave to the crowd; but they certainly gave us a tremendous roll of applause as we passed along the entire parade route. When you have to concentrate on the actions of six horses continuously, it sure keeps you busy. I can hold all six lines in one hand and drive that way for miles out on the desert country; but there in that parade, I didn't dare to double the six lines in one hand. But I did find time as we went by the President's reviewing booth to reach up with my right hand full of lines and grab the brim of my sombrero, tipped my hat to the President; and then jerked it right back in place.

Our horses drive with a really light rein; and what little slack I'd given them in reaching for my hat, was enough to let them start to move out; so when I replaced my hat, I was in a hurry to get my right hand back in its proper working position. I almost jerked my hat down over my eyebrows in my haste, but the horses hardly swerved and no one but I knew how touchy they were that day.

When we came to the end of the parade route, the bands all turned down a side street, and all the horse outfits continued on ahead. It was high time I let our coach horses out to trot and relax a bit. It didn't take us long to catch up with the horse outfit that was up ahead of us a ways. It was the Mounted Cavalry Division from Fort Carson, Colorado! They galloped along ahead of us, two abreast, for a ways. Then, at a command, they split into two single file columns , one on either side of the street, and motioned us on up amongst them. I talked to the officer in charge and we all agreed we'd travel together in style. For about a half mile or more, they escorted us in true western fashion at a good pace, on through D.C. and back to our waiting trucks. That was almost as big a thrill to be escorted in that manner as driving in the parade had been.

We finally got everything back to the racetrack and bedded down for the night. Then Jack Thompson took the whole crew of 26 of us out to dinner. You can't guess what the main topic of conversation was during dinner. We were all simply amazed to have come that far; put that much effort together on everybody's part, and then had such a good parade. As I mentioned before, the line of applause from the spectators that followed our outfit down Pennsylvania Avenue was pure proof that to us that almost everybody liked and appreciated seeing our display of the "Old West" brought back to life in front of their eyes.

The parade was over. It took another week of letting down and traveling through the winter blizzards to get home; but all that time, if we weren't discussing the greatest parade that any of us had ever been in; then we were making plans for when we hope we might return again in another four years. I doubt there would be a member of our 26 person crew that would refuse a return offer.

Apacheland

I smile to myself when sitting in the warm up area, getting ready to go into the arena at a horse show. Little do the people realize who walk by and observe our stagecoach horses standing hipshot with their heads below their withers, that "that is training," and not an indication of their true spirit. No, they are not standing that way because they are old, worn out, or cold-blooded horses. Some show people seem to feel that if it doesn't take six footmen hanging on to a dancing, rearing, head slinging horses, that they have no life, no spirit.

It's all in the training. Our horses have learned to relax when they have the opportunity, because they have grown up learning to work as they developed into full grown, muscular, well trained, gentle horses.

At a given command, they can all be in a controlled gallop in less time than it takes to tell about it. Many a time, we have done just that! In certain shows and movies, they must stand still with no holders close to them, and then leave at a gallop just by a jingle of the lines or a whistle. It takes lots of training and driving to teach them to behave properly.

All our stagecoach horses are broke to ride, and have been used under saddle about as much as in harness.

Take Romeo and Rebel. They are our lead team. They're half-brothers. Rebel, one year older, is the gentlest thing you ever saw. He's always had a gentle nature, but don't let that mis-guide you. I think he's bucked every one of my kids off a time or two. When one of the kids would get smart with him, he'd bed them down; then stand with his head lowered, ears pointing forward, with big soft eyes smiling. My oldest gal broke him to ride bareback, without a thing on his head or neck. I've seen her many a time, riding full speed through the sagebrush chousing cows, with Rebel handling better than most horses under saddle and bridle.

Romeo was different, from the day he was born. He's always been an independent cuss. For years, the only thing really good about him, was he couldn't buck very hard. He has bucked me off though.

That happened one time about noon, after moving a herd of cattle about 15 miles already since about 3:30 that morning. The more tired he'd get, the more apt he'd want to buck. I suppose for several years after I broke him to harness, I'd have to lay him down and tromp on his neck about twice a year to remind him who was supposed to be boss of our outfit. That sounds bad, but it doesn't hurt them, only they learn what isn't acceptable behavior.

He became one of the best lead horses, ever. He's always there when I need him! Anywhere I ask that lead team to go, they'll attempt it. But they are still horses, and sometimes they'll shy around at nothing, and other times they have real good excuses.

We were hauling tourists up at Apacheland one fall. I really don't blame those guys for shying. I would have myself, or maybe I boogered and caused it all.

There was a large crowd of Air Force men and women out for an evening party. We started taking rides out in our stagecoach after dark, out across our desert route. We left out of the upper end of town, heading up country ¾ of a mile. Then we circled to the left on a gentle downhill grade. When we were about even with the lower end of town, we'd circle to the left again over some rolling low hills and come into town at a slow gallop. It was about a two mile ride that the people really seemed to enjoy, and thoroughly get the feel of a stagecoach ride.

There were three or four couples on the first ride. They asked, if they paid extra, if I would take them on that ride at a fast gallop.

I'm like my horses. They like to run, and I like to drive them that way.

"You bet!" was my answer.

"As soon as we get all the other rides finished, if you still want a fast one, come on back."

I think we hauled 8 or 9 loads around. It was getting cold and late. I hadn't seen any of the fast riders, and was looking forward to putting up the horses on what I figured was the last load.

Sure enough, though, those guys had been keeping score in the saloon, and knew when to show up.

"You bet, get on. We need a run to warm us up," and run we did!

The gunfighters had put on a show early in the evening, in the street, in which they used an old wooden board outhouse.. When they got through, they just left it there, in my way, almost in the middle of the street, where I came into town. I came in on a side street and tuned to the left, up the main drag. The outhouse was on Main Street to my left, as I turned up Main. I guess everyone in the saloon knew we were going for a fast ride and were waiting for our return.

Just as we raced through the last dip before coming in, one of the gunfighters looked out and noticed the outhouse, and decided he'd better get it out of the way. The way they moved it, was by getting inside of it, and grabbing the two hand-holds on the inside, pick it up, and walk with it.

Well, Mr. Outhouse Mover had just got inside when he heard us galloping around the corner. He got boogered and tried to run with it, just as Romeo and Rebel reached it. All at once, this damned outhouse jumped about a foot in the air and started bouncing across the street!

The wreck was on! Those leaders wanted no part of that runaway outhouse!! And they sold out to the right! The hotel steps, about three feet high at the top, came down at a diagonal into the street. The hotel was across the street, and to the left of the cross street that we used when we came into town.

This immediately put them to the right of my leaders, as soon as I started my turn into town. We'd made enough of the turn to put the steps there in the way of my lead team stampeding to the right.

We were going too damn fast to get stopped, so I threw the slack in the lines to them, and they completely leaped over those steps, which were about 6 or 8 feet wide. I fell back on the lines and like to broke the break lever off, jabbing down on it. We slid to a stop at the dead end of the street, missing the steps with the other horses and the coach!

We backed back down on Main, and gently coaxed Romeo and Rebel, that the capsized outhouse over next to the high rail across the street, wouldn't come get them again.

Like I said, I didn't blame them; as I think I was about as badly boogered as they were! The passengers thought it was an exciting ride, with a whale of an ending!

I could write a whole book about the scrapes those two horses have got me into and out of; and I might just do it later, but right now I got to go back and tell about the personalities of the rest of the hitch.

Horse Whispering

Years ago, when we lived up at Westcliffe, Colorado one summer, we were making a living hauling tourists in our stagecoach and six horse hitch. There were several dude ranches in the area. I had made a deal with several of them to bring our coach to their ranch one day a week, (different day of the week for each ranch), and haul their guests for a specified price.

We had exciting happenings at almost every ranch, sometime during the day. One ranch we worked at had a large group of college kids there one week. One told me they were all working on their college thesis, whatever that is. That guy wanted to know if he could ride up on top with me, on the "shotgun" seat, which was fine with me.

It was a good ride on an all dirt back road with some dips and curves, as we were up high in those Rocky Mountains. We hit a good gallop for them on the flatter sections.

After we'd gone two or three or more miles, my "shotgun rider" asked me, "How do you steer the horses?" He'd seen the leather lines in my hands, but not seen any movements in my hands or arms.

He didn't know a good "skinner" (mule skinner) could manipulate the lines between his fingers to guide the horses, without moving his hands and arms like you see in the movies when the stagecoach is traveling.

I thought for a minute or two before answering. Then, grinning to myself, I asked, "You know about this E.S.P. malarkey?

"Yes, of course," was his answer"

"Well, you see that near lead horse up there, that's the one on the left side, out in the lead. He and I have a good understanding ESP, and he communicates to the other horses what is expected of them."

With a surprised, but interested stare at me, he wanted to know if I could communicate that way with all horses.

"No, was my reply. Sometimes I go through 100 horses before I find one I can do that with." I thought that college boy bought it all, and used it for his college thesis

Two or three years or more later, Robert Redford came out with "The Horse Whisperer" movie, or whatever it was called. After that, several horse events we went to, had a "horse whisperer".

"Would you suspicion I might have started that whole shebang?"

Introduction To Old Tucson

Today, June 14, 2018, is Flag Day.

That is quite a while since last I wrote what we'd been doing.

As I mentioned before, in the fall of 1978, we moved to Apacheland, near Apache Junction in central Arizona.

A year later, when the owner wanted to change the Old West theme of the place, to a modern disco type of entertainment, we moved on again. I was hired to manage a small ranch in the mountains a little southeast of Oracle, Arizona, and about an hour's drive from Tucson.

The new owners planned on developing a large western ranch resort there, and wanted me to run the horse activities. They went bottoms up before getting it all put together. We stayed there about four years.

Another change. Went back to cowboying on a large ranch north of Oracle. A year later, after I discovered and mentioned to the cowboss, that he had misappropriated the contents of a large double deck cattle truck, I was invited to move on.

Because we had quite a few head of broke stagecoach horses, we were asked to come help through the Thanksgiving holiday, hauling tourists at Old Tucson. In the past four years, we had done some commercials and movie work there. We were supposed to be there only for those three days.

I guess that we must have impressed the head man, Bob Shelton, manager of Old Tucson, as he asked us to stay on for a while. Almost seven years later, we quit the stagecoach hauling tourists at Old Tucson. Bob Shelton retired, and we didn't care too much for the new manager. Anyone who has a sign on his desk that says, "Just Call Me God," doesn't rank too high in my think tank!

We had gotten acquainted with many of the movie and commercials people while there, and they liked us; so we continued in the business, furnishing equipment such as wagons, buggies, and coaches, as well as horses and cattle, and good wranglers that we knew.

Morgans In The Movies

I first got acquainted with the Morgan horse in the 1940's, near Santa Rosa, California. It was 4th of July and a bunch of us cowboys had a few days off; so we were at a rodeo. Part of the entertainment was the stagecoach holdup, with six head of Morgan horses, and lots of shooting. I never forgot that scene, and it influenced my life to the point that I finally got my own stagecoach and six head of good Morgan horses by 1973.

Since then I've seen and used many registered Morgans and many half-Morgans. We used many in the late 70's s and right on through to today. In the 80's, we started working in Arizona and New Mexico in the movies. I thought I might share some of the scenes and events that happened.

On one movie, the hero was on Roulette, a Registered Morgan mare. He was chasing an outlaw who was afoot, up the street. The outlaw ducked through this narrow door which was right beside a large window that was about four feet wide by five feet high. The outlaw didn't make his escape because the hero came at a gallop; turned Roulette and jumped her right through the glass window, and captured the outlaw. No one but us knew how we had trained that mare for that stunt, and she really loved to jump. She was our youngest daughter's 4H horse and Wendy went to State on her in thirteen classes, including Jumping.

We started with an open hole where the window was and daylight in the room with no obstacles in the way. Roulette jumped right through the open window. After several rehearsals we placed the balsa wood cross panels in the hole which disintegrated easily on contact. Before the actual stunt, the sugar glass panels were put in place. They disintegrated easily also on the jump. It sure looked good, and no retakes were required.

In another movie, in the middle of a cold night, the outlaws got into a gunfight. There was a wagonload of hay with a team of Morgans, Holly-Ann and Rebel, hooked to it. In the fight a lighted kerosene lantern was thrown at someone. It missed the intended victim and lit in the wagon, spilling kerosene on the hay and catching it on fire. The shooting and the billowing flames spooked the horses. They took off at a full gallop! At the end of the street there was a hangman's platform and noose which was intended for use the next day. Just before reaching the scaffold, a front wheel of the wagon struck some obstacle causing the tongue to break just ahead of the axle. This set the horses loose. The wagon in high flames swerved and crashed into the scaffold, cameras running! The director let it burn for quite awhile (probably only a few minutes) before he yelled "Cut!" The fire was put out and the burning hay was raked out from <u>over me!</u> I was 'blind driving' under the burning hay!

Like I mentioned earlier, it was a cold January night in the Santa Fe country. When everybody was concerned if I was OK, it reminded me of a song about Alaska. I think it was called 'The Cremation of Sam McGee'. A frozen miner was chunked into a furnace to get rid of him. When they opened the furnace door to see if he was cooked yet, he raised up and said, "Shut the door, this is the first time I've been warm since I left Tennessee!" Naturally, I had to answer the movie people with, "Who in the devil put out the fire? That's the first time I've been warm since I left Tucson!" Oh yeah, Holly-Ann and Rebel were picked up by my outrider wranglers up ahead in the dark.

Houlihan was also a registered Morgan. My friend, Dave Cass, the stunt coordinator, always picked out a good running scene, with shooting off the horse for himself. Of course I mounted him on one of our best. One day Dave says to me that he needed a different horse. "What's wrong with Houlihan?," I asks him. Dave replied, "All he wants to do is run to the wild country."

"Dave", I says, "Have you ever got on him that you didn't leave at a full gallop, and on return come to a hard stop, bail off, and hand him to a wrangler? If you get on him gently and ride around slow, then gallop some, and ride reasonable again. Then talk to him and pet his neck before you get off. I think you'll find out he's the best you can get. Houlihan's problem is he is full of ambition and he likes to run. When he sees you coming, he's like a kid that sees what he likes best. Goody, goody! Here comes good old Dave so we can go on a good run!"

Dave followed my idea. The next movie Dave got on Houlihan and rode for a few minutes before running in his scene. Houlihan performed magnificently. Dave wouldn't ride any other horse than Houlihan after that,

I raised and trained him, as well as all our other horses. Some of you might remember Rebel when he won the trotting race at the Plymouth, California Morgan horse show in 1976. We had just finished our Bi-Centennial stagecoach trip from St. Jo, Missouri to Sacramento, California, driving the Central Overland Trail.

Romeo and Rebel, both registered Morgans, were our lead team of the six up stagecoach hitch. They appeared in many movies, commercials, and parades from coast to coast. Our original 6-up hitch:

**Sherwood Romeo,   Eedahow Rebel
Sherwood Roulette,   Royal Brightstar (Robbie)
Bandito (half Morgan/Quarterhorse),   Houlihan**

Destry, A Good Horse

Back in the sixties, I bought my wife a beautiful, well-built Hancock mare. She was gentle as a dog, but I'm telling you, if I hadn't known her and was cutting her out of a cavvy; when I roped her, I would have become pretty leery. When you roped her, she'd come right out to you with the whites of her eyes showing, her ears laid back, and a look like she was going to eat you alive.

More than once, I walked up and bailed on her bareback with just the lass rope around her neck and rode out away from the herd. She was actually all bluff.

This yarn isn't about her though, but one of her colts. It needed some of her background. Also, a side note. When I was growing up, the word colt according to Webster's 1935 dictionary defined it as a baby horse, so everyone used the terms stud colt or horse colt for males, and filly for females.

We bred this mare to our Morgan stud, Jackson. From 1968 to 1979 she produced eight horse colts and two fillies. Cisco, the last of her brood, was born in 1977.

This story is about one of Cisco's brothers, named Destry, born in 1974. I started him as three-year old, and he soon learned all the cues a good cavalry horse needed to know to stay in proper formation and perform in any drill, as well as normal ranch cowboy activities of roping, moving cattle, sidestepping to open gates, etc.

I traded him to our second cowboy daughter, Tammie, who was involved in rodeo activities for several years. By the time he was four or five, his Hancock blood started to the surface. Tammie was working full time; so she didn't have enough time to spend on Destry. I finally bought him back from her for a thousand dollars.

We were doing movies pretty steady about that time; so I started riding him hard, and put him in as a cast horse. He was a beautiful well-built brown-black like his mother, with a large star; a real eye-catcher. I don't recall what was Destry's movie debut, but one of the first big jobs was a Kemper Cavalry commercial at Monument Valley in Arizona.

We had about 18 cavalry men in the unit. Tony Brubaker, a Hollywood stunt man, was one of the officers in the lead. Tony's not one of those little light guys. The first day he wore out two of my bigger stout horses. (We were doing a lot of hard riding.) Destry was young and feisty, so; "What the Hell?" I'd test his mettle. Tony rode him the rest of the shoot and stayed right out in the lead where he was supposed to be. He was a pretty fair horseman.

We did lots of hard riding and different maneuvers in front of the camera. One of them was rather exciting. We were in the sand dunes area when the director asked me to take a ride with his crew to look over a possible shoot.

We circled around and came up perpendicular to a long hogback ridge of sand. The slope on the camera side was steep. As steep as I've ever seen a sand hill.

He'd like to see the heads and shoulders of the unit in twos come galloping along on the back side of the ridge, and at the given command, the column would make a 90 degree right turn and come over the ridge, evenly spaced abreast, and ride (or slide!) to the bottom. Then make a 90 degree left turn, fall back into perfect formation and gallop out of frame. From top to bottom, the sand dune was about 60 feet high and probably at least 60 degrees steep! It would take a little setting up, but I told him we could give it to them that way.

I rode back to the unit and told them to stay exactly where they were; not to look over the hogback as the director wanted a clean unmarked shot. I would take another wrangler and we'd make a trail on the back side where the crew was, wide enough and packed down where two men could gallop side by side. I explained that when Tony and his partner reached a spot where there was a surviving soapweed bush, that whichever was closest to the ridge would stop and start his right turn so the whole column appeared abreast, evenly spaced. They were not to stop at any time. just turn and ride over the top. I didn't want anyone looking over it until they were committed and couldn't turn back; (which I didn't tell them.) At the bottom they were to turn left as a unit and canter out of frame in formation.

It was magnificent and went over almost perfect, with some very startled expressions as they dove over the top and saw what they were going down.

There was a greasewood bush sticking up out of the sand about a horse length before the bottom. One of the horses slid astraddle of it and caused him to turn sideways, pointing in the opposite direction as he hit the flat land. He had a good hand on him that picked up his front end, pivoted him around, and went right into proper formation, and the unit galloped out of frame perfectly, with Destry packing Tony in the lead.

I used Destry in several shoots, and he always did good. We were on a movie filming up on Rosemont Ridge, southeast of Tucson, when they informed me one of the stars of that Desperado episode would show up in the afternoon. He was an experienced horseman and needed a good horse. At noon, they said he would be late getting there, but they had a stand-in to take his place at rehearsing the scene so as to be ready for the star. The stand-in was a local roper cowboy, and apparently Destry didn't approve of him. He was belligerent all afternoon. A couple times I thought he was going to blow up and buck.

Finally the star showed up. I was quite concerned, not knowing him, and thinking about the way Destry had been acting. I got rid of the stand-in, and was holding Destry when the star walked up. I introduced them like you would two prize fighters in a ring. To the star, "This is your horse, Destry, and Destry, this is your new boss."

Destry looked him up and down; then stepped up closer and rubbed his forehead and face on the man's stomach. That man stepped on Destry and rode off like he'd known him a long time.

Things don't always go smooth. One day he came to me and said he had to have a different horse for the next scene.

Why? I asked.

He won't stand still. This next scene calls for lots of dialogue, and I can't be moving around. I thought for a minute, then came up with something like this.

"You're an experienced horseman, with a daughter in world champion dressage and jumping competition; so you surely know a bunch about horses. Your trouble is that Destry knows all the dressage cues, and every time you wiggle and squirm on him he thinks you are cueing him to move. If you want him to stand still, you sit still."

I'd put him on his mettle, so he agreed to try it.

In the movie, this star was the #2 outlaw business man, who had been caught by the good guys, stripped to his long johns, and sent back to town with a message for his boss, the #1 Head Honcho.

   As he rode into town, a crowd of 50 or more of the townsmen gathered completely around him, jeering and yelling, pointing fingers and laughing at him. He came to a stop outside the hotel, looking up at the second floor balcony where his boss was staring down at him.

   The star had a disgusted look on his face, and Destry had the same expression. The dialogue went on for a half hour or more, what with cuts, retakes, and slight changes before the scene was finished. The man sat perfectly still with his body and legs, and Destry stood at perfect attention. He never moved a single foot out of the stance he stopped in, until it was over and the star rode off. I thought to myself, "Good horse."

   That star really liked Destry, and wanted to buy him at the end of the movie. I said, "He's not for sale." He kept after me, insisting I put a price on him. I finally did. Fifteen thousand dollars. I figured it was so high I wouldn't have to worry about it. The man came within a hair of whipping out the money right then. If he had, I'd probably tried to figure a way out of the deal.

   Destry had a sense of humor of his own. We were on a shoot up at Page, Arizona doing one of those women warrior scenes. In a box canyon on rehearsal, I led Destry in. The man star and the lady warrior meet. The warrior, well-endowed, wearing scant buckskins with fringe 6 inches long hanging down over her protruding front quarters, stepped up close, a foot or so in front of Destry. He stood there looking at her, then stuck his nose out and fluffed up

that fringe hanging off that left front protruding part, right up over her shoulder, and nuzzling the tip of that buckskin as
he did that. 25 or more men saw him do it. It brought out some exciting comments. I turned to the crew and said, "I taught him everything he knows." Most every man there envied Destry's position.

    Today, February 2005, we're here at the Eaves Movie Ranch in New Mexico, filming
"Into The West". There is a short train track with 3 cattle cars and a box car that were brought here and set up for a movie we did here quite a few years back. I remember that scene well.

    The two stars come out of a saloon as the posse is galloping into town after them. The stars vault to their saddles for their getaway. Both cross streets ahead of them are blocked with horsemen and cattle. There is a cattle train crossing the street up ahead. The boardwalk on the right side of the street slopes up to the loading dock, right level with the train doors. A cattle car approaches with both doors open, one on each side, so you can see clear through to the country on the far side. The riders see this, and jump their horses onto the boardwalk at a gallop. They reach the open cattle car door at the right place; go into and through the car, jumping to the ground on the far side and making their getaway.

    The train was moving at 7.5 MPH, and the horses were at a good gallop. We had a big truck with a good winch on the front end pulling the train cars. The driver had a tachometer to show the motor speed. We rehearsed the stunt for two weeks starting with the cars standing still; then gradually moving, and increasing until we were at maximum speed.

On the last rehearsal the day before filming the stunt, I was on the street where I could watch both the train and the horses. Those train car door openings are only 5 or 6 feet wide, which goes by pretty quick at 7.5 MPH. We had to put Whang's head (the second horse) right up to the lead rider in order for his rear to clear the moving entrance. Rehearsal was on. Here came the riders, 30 feet from the contact site. Destry's nose was extended ahead of him, angled toward the approaching open doorway. His ears pointed right at that door. As the contact point came closer, his neck straightened out perfectly ahead of him as he entered the doorway.

When we filmed it, it was a beautiful perfectly performed stunt. The heroes made their getaway again.

A couple years ago, while we were on the 4th remake of "The Alamo", my brother who was taking care of our ranch, called me and said Destry had laid down and died peacefully in his sleep. He got our backhoe and buried him. **Goodbye old friend**.

The reason for this yarn. The other day one of the movie cowboys, which on this job happen to be almost all ranch hands, stated he'd never had a really good horse.

The thought ran through my think tank, that I must be one of the lucky ones, because I've had several "good horses".

Destry was one of the best, so I had to tell a little about him, although I could probably ramble on enough more stories of his life to write a whole book.

Suntan is on the 'near swing'

Smart Horse - Suntan

    Some domesticated horses know and understand many more things about humans than humans do about horses. Suntan, a registered Morgan mare that we raised and broke to ride and drive in harness, was one. She wasn't a beautiful mare; that is, she didn't have perfect conformation, especially for the registered Morgan that she was, but she had a personality all her own. She was probably the easiest riding horse I was ever on. I think you could have set a glass of water on her hips or withers, and trot her down the road without sloshing a drop out.

    For some reason unknown to us, she disliked our son, Kip. I don't know what caused it. Every time he'd work around her, she'd try to bite or kick at him. She wasn't playing, but she didn't bite or kick at him viciously. I could crawl between her legs or scratch her on the belly, and she'd just look at me with soft eyes. I don't remember ever seeing her kick at another person, though one time she had a good opportunity.

In the early 80's, we were doing a Hubba Bubba Bubble Gum commercial down by the Rio Rico area, with our stagecoach. It was supposed to be a "hold-up" of some kind by mounted outlaws. I think the title was, "The Gum Slinger." When the hero steps out of the coach and busts a big bubble all to smithereens, the outlaws' horses stampede. One of the robbers was supposed to perform a high roll-back and head across the river where he'd get shot off his horse in the water.

He wasn't what I'd call an excellent horse stuntman. When he did his high rollback, he pulled his horse so high, that he fell over backwards, throwing the rider quite a ways. When he quit falling and rolling, he wound up right behind Suntan, lying on his side with his head right behind her rear heels!

All this time I was talking to my horses with the lines, and telling Suntan, "No, no Suntan, don't you kick the poor dumb idiot." He was just lying there, still not trying to get away. Suntan was in the near swing position (left side of the middle team of the six up hitch). Suntan turned her head around to the right side and looked down toward her heels at the feller lying there. She looked directly at his head; her eyes focused and her ears pointed directly at him. Then, believe it or not, she raised her head up, looking directly at me, with her upper lip curled up like in a grin. It was just as if she had said, "Did you ever see such a numbskull as that?"

She held that pose several moments, until that dude got up and out of the way. Then she straightened up, shook her head, and stood perfectly still. That's what I'd call a very intelligent horse!

'Stagecoach' Movie

How many fellers do you suppose have driven a stagecoach with six fiery horses lunging ahead of it for a hundred miles?

Not too many that are still alive, would be my guess; and that's a thrill that has no equal, as far as I'm concerned. Living a wild cowboy life in the West, I've had my share of them. Nothing I know of has had the lasting pleasure of the thrill of shaking the slack in the lines to six charging runners with a good coach under you.

 I had looked forward to the following words, spoken to me the other day, but saddened to know another beloved era had come to an end. The words were "That's a final wrap. We have every little bit we needed to put it all together now!"

It all started a couple months ago when I was called up to the office to meet some people who were planning to film a television movie of the epic John Wayne movie, "Stagecoach to Lordsburg." They were interested to know if I had enough good horses, and the ability to do the stunt driving to film the movie.

I was in a hectic turmoil for the next month. One report, I'd get, would be, "they were still interested in coming here, and the next news would be they were thinking of going elsewhere."
Finally, I was on Cloud 9; they were coming here! "Yes, they'd use my horses and most of all - yes I'd be doing the stunt driving, doubling John Schneider."

We'd need three distinctly different hitches, and a fourth running hitch to double the #3 chase hitch. No problem. I had more than 24 stagecoach horses, enough for the posse, the Indians, the cavalry, wranglers, scouts, and town horses. If I was short, and needed more, I knew where I could pick them up.

Also, I had to continue to run my horse business at Old Tucson, which required another 20 head. The whole movie took 24 stagecoach horses, 30 Indians horses, 30 cavalry horses, 15 town horses, 8 posse horses, 6 wrangle horses, 2 "Ringo" horses, 2 "Ringo and Dallas" horses, 2 scout horses, 4 army ambulance horses, 4 "nester" ambush wagon horses; for a grandtotal of 127 'horse days'. We were able to use some of the horses in different scenes, but we still used about 90 head of different horses to film the whole movie!

I won't say it was an easy film to work. We were very busy with the horses almost the entire shoot, but yet it was not a hard film to work. We had practically no 'prep' time, but because all our stagecoach horses are used regularly and are in good driving shape, made things easier.

Our one problem was in deciding how to pair up the horses, to give them three distinctively different hitches, and a double for the fourth hitch. Also, the lead team on the #3 hitch had to be well broke, stout, dependable, proven horses, as well as runners; to insure the safety of the stunt men. They would be doing their stunt down on the wheel tongue between those horses, at a full gallop! No simple thing, in the least.

To complicate matters, almost all our horses are sorrels, but of different shades. Our # 1 hitch was made up of mostly light colored and reddish solid colored horses. The # 2 hitch all had blaze faces. Numbers 3 and 4 were made up of the chestnuts and darker sorrels except for the near wheelers which were light yellowish sorrels, full brothers. Number 3 near wheel horse was the big stout gentle one for the stunts, and # 4 near wheel was a runner. The 'off' wheelers for both #3 and #4 were dark bay and reddish horses; one was gentle, the other, a hard runner.

We were fortunate in having several sets of full brothers that were almost identical, to double for different shots through the show. The horse that Ringo rode up close, was a full brother to the one Kip, (our son), rode, doubling Ringo, on the hard rides at a distance. Up close, we have to look close to tell them apart, and we raised them!

I rented 10 head of pinto horses for color in the Indians band, and with our sorrels and roans stirred up in the band, they really looked good. We rented some posse horses, but used our own wrangle horses.

The movie made a deal with the Fort Huachuca Cavalry unit as a group, and they brought their own horses for the big cavalry encampment. We used our own horses for the cavalry escort group of eight.

The army ambulance 4-up was ours, as well as most of the town horses.

As I mentioned before, we didn't have much prep time. We moved to Mescal Sunday and started filming Monday morning. I had not had a chance to even look the stagecoach over, that was brought from Hollywood for the exterior and chase shots. They did use my Concord coach for the interior shots.

So, we were a little slow getting started Monday morning. I said I felt like an Indianapolis race driver, arriving at the track after the starting flags had been raised, and saying, "O.K. which one is my race car?"

We put her together and made it work. The next day, we got a breather for awhile, as I was able to make some changes and adjustments good enough to run the rest of the movie.

Our Stagecoach Harness

We have a six-up set of stagecoach harness that has a world of history to it.

It was designed by Ben Holladay, somewhere in the 1850's or there abouts. Ben Holladay ran the mail stagecoach route from Salt Lake City, Utah to St. Joseph, Missouri for two years before he sold out to Wells Fargo.

Ben was one of the instigators of the northern route from Sacramento to St. Joe that ran from the 1858's to the 1869's, when the trans-continental railroad was completed. He had lots of experience and knew what it took to keep a coach moving rapidly. One was to have relay stations as close as 15 miles together where it was possible. Some of the western runs were longer due to terrain, water, and Indians.

Ben knew that the less weight a horse packed that the farther and faster he could travel. Ben designed his own harness as light as possible. Hames, tugs, backband with belly band, a back strap, lines and bridles was all that was needed. Ben's harness weighs less than 15 pounds per horse.

E.R. Simpson was a stagecoach collector and driver. When I knew him & his son, Meade, they had a ranch near Sloughhouse, Calif. E.R. had a coach barn more than an acre large, full of coaches. At one time I was told that E.R. had owned at least one coach off from every stagecoach company that ran in California.

In 1948 Meade hooked up a 6 horse hitch to a coach and drove it up to where his dad was. E.R. got on and took the lines. Meade got off. E.R. started out like a coach ought to start, and the horses must have been feeling good. They went through a run to a runaway.

I discovered a long time later that the outside check to a horse broke as E.R. pulled up hard to control the hitch. With an outside check broken that put a hard pull out on the other horse causing the lead team to swing hard to that side. A coach was designed to run hard forward with about only a 30 degree turn. When the hitch swung hard to that side it drove the front wheel hard into the side of the coach; that flipped the coach over instantly. That wreck killed E.R.. Meade was so disgustedly hurt that he put the harness in a big box and sealed it shut tight.

I knew about the wreck and what Meade had done with the harness. Several times when I stopped by to visit with Meade and asked what he was ever going to do with that harness, I could get no answer from him. I knew Meade, quite well.

In the stagecoach collection he had the original coach that Black Bart held up on Copperopolis Mountain. That holdup was the last of his hold ups. He was caught and convicted and ended his holdup career. Several years ago two of my Sacramento horse and movie people decided to make a movie of that Black Bart holdup. Meade let us use the original Black Bart holdup coach and we filmed it on the spot where Black Bart had originally done his last holdup.

We couldn't haul the coach more than 2 or 3 miles from the set. The old original road was washed bad, and besides, a large lake covered the road in the valley that the coach came up out of. I had more experience with stagecoaches than the movie men had so I had to direct most of the holdup action. Meade was up there with us, so when we got through I tried persuading Meade to get on the coach with me and ride back down to the automobiles.

When he finally got on, he looked at me sorta odd and says, "Red, this is the first stagecoach ride I've been on since 1948."

Sometime later I stopped by his house, they told me Meade was down at the barn. We hadn't been together for quite a while, so we had quite a bit of visiting to do. Nothing was said about the harness. Finally Meade suggested we go up to the house and have a beer or two. That sure sounded good to me on that hot afternoon.

We drank our beers and were sitting there when Meade came out with "Red let's take your pickup back down to the barn and throw that harness in it." We did that and I've had it, using it in commercials and movies ever since.

I had to repair a few straps and replace the old bridles and the driving lines. That's how I discovered what caused the awful wreck and killed his dad.

I had the harness appraised by one of the Antique Fair people a few years ago. I told him I didn't have any written information on the harness, but I had known the Simpsons and the harness a good many years and told him what I knew about the harness being designed by Ben Holladay, and how I got it.

The agent said he'd appraised quite a bit of harness so he was familiar with all the working parts of one. He said he'd appraise our harness at between 50 & 80 thousand dollars. Also he felt sure if we took it to a large antique sale with my story about it, that it would sell for a minimum of $20,000 cash.

We still have the harness and have never tried to sell it.

Hatch, New Mexico

In our work for the movies, we saw some interesting places. One of those was Hatch, New Mexico, Chili Capital of the world!

Recently, I was taking a semi-load of wagons to Santa Fe, New Mexico, to use on a movie up there. I had some letters I wanted to mail. I knew that the Post Office in Hatch was located in the center of town right on the main drag, and there was room to stop and park my truck in front of it. After mailing my letters, I was checking the tie-down straps on the wagons and re-adjusting them. A large SUV with a man and wife and full of kids, stopped to look at the wagons. After visiting for a few minutes, I casually mentioned how I liked Hatch, the chili capital of the world, and that I usually picked up an assortment of chili when I came through.

He responded, "We have a business here in town; so stop when you come back through and I'll have a batch ready for you". I hated to have to tell him, "Thank you for the offer, but no thank", because I was returning on the northern route. I said maybe I'd see him on my next trip through.

It is quite a sight to see all the different chilis hanging in the store fronts, and the other chili assortments there as you pass through that small town.

Outstanding Events In My Life

We performed the last stagecoach bank holdup in the United States in the fall of 1977 in Louisville, Kentucky! With our stagecoach pulled by our six horse hitch, we hauled the robbers to the bank and pulled up in front of it. Our holdup men performed the robbery, and we made a getaway in the coach. Of course we were caught and apprehended before we got out of town; and the bank employees were thrilled to death to be a part of the whole shebang. We did it to advertise Monty Montana Jr.'s Wild West Show, performing there at the time.

I've driven ten head of horses or mules ahead of five wagons, hooked together properly, in California and Arizona. We also took the grand prize in a parade with over 400 horse entries in the Tucson, Arizona Vaqueros Rodeo Parade.

I qualified for thirteen years in the SAG (Screen Actors Guild) movie union, mostly doubling for an actor who wasn't a skilled coach driver, or a good rider ahorseback. One of the most interesting movies to me was where an actor had to double me in a movie. It's usually the other way around.

When we did "Stagecoach To Lordsburg," the third version, {John Wayne did the first one about 1939}, John Schneider played the part of the coach driver. He wasn't as "old western looking," "quote," as I was. He had to go to 'Make Up' every morning to look like me. I went to 'Make Up' once to trim

"STAGECOACH" 1986
JOHN SCHNEIDER   JOHNNY CASH   KRIS KRISTOFFERSON

the long growing hairs from my beard to keep it even. Usually it's the reverse, the stunt man doubles the actor. It was quite a thrill for me for one of the leading actors to have to double me!

After the film was produced, Marge and I were up in Bob Shelton's Old Tucson office on some business. When I saw a poster showing John Schneider, as the coach driver, and Johnny Cash as the "shotgun" rider, I studied it for a while, before I called Marge's attention to look at it. She studied it for a while before she said, "It's good, but what's wrong?" John had a nice smile, and his teeth were all even and good looking. In the poster, just enough of the teeth were showing, to show one front middle tooth broken off at a 45% angle. I had a front tooth broken off at a 45% angle, from a fight years ago. No one but us knew the makeup man had us looking so much alike, you couldn't tell us apart. We got a good laugh out of this.

On one of Kenny Roger's movies, I was driving a team for background movement. One horse was a black horse; the other was white or light gray. I had two different jackets and two different hats in my wagon. I would drive across on "Action!" with the black horse showing to the camera, and while I was turning around at the other end, I would change wardrobe and hats. Again, on "Action," I would come back the other way with a different wardrobe and a white horse showing, also, a different wagon as one side was painted a different color from the other. Movie Magic! At the end of the movie, crossing the street behind Kenny Rogers for a still shot, my team was on a run, caught mostly in the air, still behind Kenny, as the credits ran. I got quite a thrill out of that when I saw the movie.

I did many driving stunts, but one that gave me a thrill, was when we planned to blow up the "gold laden" War Wagon. Several people involved with the movie came to me, worried that the Humane Society would not allow us to blow up the war wagon with the horses hooked to it, and they would be there that day to watch the whole thing. I went up and got acquainted with them. I said we had to rehearse the actual stunt in slow motion before we did it. I explained how we planned to do it. We would bring the horses up and put them in place with nothing hooked up. We'd have six wranglers ahorseback, one beside each horse. On" Action," they'd lead the horses in a walk, in proper position, through the scene area to the safe area beyond. Then we'd bring them back to position, and this time we'd leave in a fast gallop through the film area to the safe area beyond sight of the camera once again.

I explained how the Special Effects man had the tongue on a quick release with the first explosion that would release the horses. There were two one-half inch thick steel bolts that attached the tongue of the wagon to the wagon box. He had a keyboard electrically hooked up. The first button blew out those bolts and turned the horses loose. If he didn't see the first flash right, he wouldn't touch any of the other buttons off, and we'd have to do it over.

The six wranglers would be in position out of frame to catch them. The six horses would run the short distance where, between the two sets of three wranglers on each side, they were waiting to pick up the loose hitch.

We rehearsed the whole thing. All good.
"Time. Everybody get set. Roll Camera."
"Action!"
I signaled my horses with the lines, and we were off!

I was driving six horses running full throttle.
BOOM!

The first explosion went off as planned, and the horses were out of there! The rest of the wagon blew! Immediately following the release of the horses, several explosions went off simultaneously with me inside. The whole back of the wagon blew to smithereens! What an explosion! The pieces went flying; some going 50 to 100 feet in the air! One of those steel bolts thrust into a tree about five feet away, and buried itself 8 inches to the hilt! It blew away two <u>one-half inch steel pins</u> that held the tongue of the coach to the axle. This turned the six horses loose, carrying the tongue with them. They went forward a short distance, and were out of sight of the camera, where they were picked up immediately by the six wranglers, still in position and totally safe.

Dick Farnsworth, a famous actor was there at the time. (My first work with Dick Farnsworth was way back in the 1940's. That was my first stagecoach robbery, and he was the driver of the stagecoach in a parade.) He came up to me after I got out of the wagon and said, "Red, you know I've been a stunt man in the movies all my life, and that was the most spectacular horse stunt I've ever seen and taken part in." It thrilled me no end.

Everything went very well, just like we planned. The Humane Society people were so impressed, they presented me with a special commendation for performing such a stunt without hurting or injuring any horse or person. We were then, and still are, very proud of that!

The Distance Between

There is a comradeship amongst a group of cowboys like no other bunch ever had.

There are thrills, excitement, and satisfaction, to the same type of work done day after day, that never become boring. Each day might be a repetition of the day before, but no two days are alike.

There's much beauty in this old world, and it can best be seen from the back of some kind of horse; be it trusty or treacherous. From the false dawn of the mornings to the red sunsets of evening, there's nothing to compare.

Most cowboys I've known weren't very religious in a church-going way, but cowboys have a spiritual togetherness with their Maker that I doubt very many other people ever come near to.

After a few years most cowboys have had so many close calls and narrow escapes that they begin to realize it all couldn't be "just luck".

But mostly, what I planned on writing about was the humor in a cowboy's life. I once heard it said, "The distance between tragedy and comedy is only the breadth of a cigarette paper."

And there's lots of both in a cowboy's life.

Adios

My Life is spent a-roaming,
A-traveling here and yon.
Though I've liked lots of places,
I'll soon be driftin' on.

I've had my share of friends,
Most of whom were true.
I hated to part with them,
But what else could I do?

I'm sort of sentimental;
I find it hard to say, "So Long."
So I usually leave with the night
Although I know it's wrong.

The good times that I've had
Are the riches of my wealth.
For I don't live in the past,
All alone by myself.

I have a vivid memory
For the things I love so well;
Of the many enjoyable incidents
Too valuable to sell.

I remember old Nevada,
Its deserts and my pals.
In New Mexico it was lonesome
Like the way a coyote howls

Oregon shall always remain
A wonderful place to me.
For I loved its sprawling deserts
And the fragrance of a Juniper tree.

Colorado with is mountains
And beauty beyond compare.
Will I forever share my heart?
With a love that I left there.

I could go on reminiscing
The happenings of the past;
But I must say, "So Long" again,
For the time is slipping fast.

So "Adios, old Pals.
"I love you all so well.
I hope our trails will cross again
Somewhere this side of "Hell!"

330

Adios Amigo. Glad to share my cowboy days with you. Hope you enjoyed reading about them as much as I enjoyed living the life.

Red Cloud

Red Cloud's 90th birthday – September 22nd, 2019 Surrounded by Family

About the Author

'Red Cloud', as he is known in the cattle country, was a working cowboy and horseman all his life. Raised in Colorado, he quit school at 15 and went to work breaking mules to drive for the ZX Ranch in Paisley Oregon, until he got hired 'on the wagon'. "All I ever wanted to be was a big ranch cowboy." The first 30 years of his life, he didn't know he could make a living if he wasn't ahorseback. He liked punching cows, riding broncs, driving fast horses. He travelled the west working on ranches, from Oregon to Idaho, Montana, Colorado, New Mexico, California, and finally Arizona; where he ended up. Near Tucson, he raised Morgan horses and got a stagecoach, and he turned his love of horses into a motion picture livestock business, appearing in such films as 'Tombstone', 'The Alamo', 'Into the West'. With his wife Margery, he raised three daughters and a son. He has several published books and stories.

About the Illustrator

Margery Wolverton was born in Omaha, Nebraska, in 1930. She attended the University of Nebraska-Omaha, graduating with a bachelor's degree in languages. She began drawing horses before kindergarten, and continues her love of making art to this day. Being married to Red since 1954 and seeing first hand the western way of life, the illustrations are her interpretations to capture those moments of the working cowboys.

www.ingramcontent.com/pod-product-compliance
Lightning Source LLC
Chambersburg PA
CBHW071804080526
44589CB00012B/678